BILLY GRAHAM

Evangelistic Association

Always Good News.

Dear Friend,

I am pleased to send you this copy of *First Words of Jesus* by Stu Epperson, Jr., founder and president of The Truth Network, with radio stations across the United States and syndicated programming on affiliates nationwide.

The first words of Jesus as recorded in Scripture reveal so much about His life, death, and ultimate purpose in coming to earth. In this book, written especially for the Christmas season, Stu invites readers to grow closer to Christ by taking a deeper look at His first words in the Bible, spoken when Jesus was 12 years old. I pray that no matter where you are in your relationship with Christ, *First Words of Jesus* helps you "*know Him and the power of His resurrection*" (Philippians 3:10, NKJV) in a new and powerful way.

For more than 65 years, the Billy Graham Evangelistic Association has worked to take the Good News of Jesus Christ throughout the world by every effective means available, and I'm excited about what God will do in the years ahead.

We would appreciate knowing how our ministry has touched your life. May God richly bless you.

Sincerely,

Franklin Graham
President

If you would like to know more about our ministry, please contact us:

IN THE U.S.:

Billy Graham Evangelistic Association
1 Billy Graham Parkway
Charlotte, NC 28201-0001
BillyGraham.org
info@bgea.org
Toll-free: 1-877-247-2426

IN CANADA:

Billy Graham Evangelistic
  Association of Canada
20 Hopewell Way NE
Calgary, AB T3J 5H5
BillyGraham.ca
Toll-free: 1-888-393-0003

FIRST WORDS OF JESUS

FROM THE CRADLE TO THE CROSS

Stu Epperson, Jr.

WORTHY
Inspired

This *Billy Graham Library Selection* special edition is published with
permission from Worthy Publishing Group.

©2016 by Stu Epperson Jr.

Published by Worthy Inspired, an imprint of Worthy Publishing Group, a division of Worthy Media, Inc., One Franklin Park, 6100 Tower Circle, Suite 210, Franklin, TN 37067.

WORTHY is a registered trademark of Worthy Media, Inc.

HELPING PEOPLE EXPERIENCE THE HEART OF GOD

eBook available wherever digital books are sold.

Library of Congress Control Number: 2016949698

For foreign and subsidiary rights, contact rights@worthypublishing.com

978-1-61795-798-7 (Jacketed Hardcover)
978-1-68397-018-7 (ITPE)
978-1-59328-581-4 (BGEA Edition)

Cover Design: Jeff Jansen | aestheticsoup.net
Interior Design and Typesetting: Bart Dawson

Printed in the United States of America

CONTENTS

Used by permission of Joni Eareckson Tada of Joni and Friends

There shall the child lie in a stall,
The child who shall redeem us all.

Hugo Jungst

To my wife, Julie, a woman of exceptional courage and Hope, our first daughter, born at Christmastime— both of you are a true gift from God.

FOREWORD

BY DR. DAVID JEREMIAH

There have been many books written on the last words of Jesus. Just a year ago, the author of this book—my friend Stu Epperson—wrote *Last Words of Jesus*, which provided a fresh encounter with Jesus as the reader explored all that Jesus said from the cross and the life-changing impact of those powerful words.

In this new book, Stuart Epperson takes us back to the beginning and examines how clearly the manger in Bethlehem led to the cross of Calvary.

Throughout the stories of Jesus's birth, each person who was there played a distinct and important role. In the Gospels, we hear from each of them, Mary and Joseph, the angels, shepherds, and the magi, even Herod. Their important words not only resonate with us after all these centuries, but also foretold much of what was to come in the life of the extraordinary Baby born in a stable.

Before Jesus was born, His mother Mary's first words, when she discovered she had been selected to bear the Son of God, were words of devotion, humility, and willingness to follow God's plan. Joseph, too, exemplified faith in God even when he certainly did not understand. And when the angels actually heralded the news, their presence terrified the shepherds, but their words gave those simple men hope as they shared how the world had changed in one moment. The magi, both in their words and their gifts, foretold Jesus's destiny.

To all of this Stu Epperson brings the detail and accuracy of a scholar and the enthusiasm and passion of someone fascinated by the intricacies and beautifully woven threads that lead ultimately to the cross and then Jesus's Resurrection. As the host of his own national talk show, Stu regularly engages with believers and seekers who want to better understand the entire story of Jesus's life and purpose. Stu has his finger on the pulse of the culture as commercialism, materialism, and popular society seem to try to deny the whole reason Christ came. The world loves the Baby in the manger, but many want nothing to do with the Man on Calvary. And it is only for Calvary that Jesus came at all.

To communicate this, the author includes a treasure trove of rich hymns and carols. These songs brilliantly magnify the central figure of the Christmas story and redemption's story—the Lord Jesus Christ.

Stu Epperson also gives us an unfiltered, honest look at how Christmas is a very difficult time of year for so many.

The world today often feels dark and frightening. Christians are persecuted throughout the nations. Evil seems to flourish and it is tempting to despair. Even shortly after Jesus was born as Emmanuel, God with us, it was a time of violence and fear as Herod struck out against the baby King. God was moving, God was working, and the Savior was already there in the midst of all that pain and turmoil. By knowing Him personally we can truly experience His peace and purpose—even in our darkest struggle.

It is only by beginning at the beginning, and taking into account the whole timeline, including the first words we actually hear from Jesus when He remained at the temple, that we clearly see His understanding of His own purpose. We know that He was always about His Father's business. From the moment the angels appeared until He rose victorious from the grave, Jesus was working to save us. From His first words to His last, Jesus's life was a tapestry of salvation and grace.

I heartily commend *First Words of Jesus* to you. Read it with those you love and give it away generously as a gift to those you want to reach with the good news of the Savior. My prayer is that this book will add a special blessing to your Christmas, and to your life—connecting you more deeply with Jesus, the One who came that we "may have life and may have it more abundantly"(John 10:10).

INTRODUCTION

No two religious symbols have been more commercialized and trivialized than the manger (Christmas) and the cross (Good Friday/Easter). One represents the greatest economic boon in modern western history. The other universally adorns necks and walls as jewelry and art's most popular merchandise.

Yet the cradle and the cross are inextricably and eternally connected. In my book *Last Words of Jesus,* the focus is on the cross and specifically what Jesus said there as He died. This book goes back to His *first* recorded words, and then further back to the remarkable beginning of His earthly life. My passion is that by the end of this book, you'll see Jesus Christ in a refreshing new light—the light of His grand entrance into this world and His grand mission, which took Him all the way to the cross.

"'The New Testament knows nothing of an incarnation which can be defined apart from its relation to atonement. . . . Not Bethlehem but Calvary is the focus of revelation, and any construction of Christianity which ignores or denies

1

this distorts Christianity by putting it out of focus.' The crucial significance of the cradle at Bethlehem lies in its place in the sequence of steps that led the Son of God to the cross of Calvary, and we do not understand it till we see it in this context."[1]

The Great Hymnal Heist

Tears dripped from my eyes and splashed the pages of the hymnal. I was at church during one of my daughters' many Christmas programs and pulled the songbook from the back of the pew in front of me. At the time, I was just finishing my first book—a very "cross focused" book—so my heart was tender to the words I read about the cross in the carols of Christmas. You see, I have been "hearing" the songs of Christmas all my life, but it wasn't until I started "listening" that everything changed. Many of the Christmas hymns we love and cherish masterfully convey the mission of Jesus and heart of Christmas. As you encounter them here, I pray you'll drink them in and let them marinate in your soul. Getting this point across to teenagers, however, proved to be another matter altogether, requiring a drastic action—one even a bit scandalous.

It was the perfect crime. If you told me when I was just a young lad that I would one day steal more than a dozen hymnals from the church sanctuary, I would have been horrified. Never, ever would I even consider such a despicable act. But times are different today as the age of the hymnbook fades more and more each year. Desperate times require desperate measures. In order to teach a Christmas lesson one Sunday, I recruited several "churched" criminals to help me in the great hymnal heist. As a result, some of our tenth graders experienced hymnal singing for the first time in their life. They were actually "singing from the same sheet of music."

The good news is that we retuned the hymnals promptly after class; the bad news is that no one missed them! The best news is why we consulted hymnals to begin with. You'll see in this book why I'm so grateful for a bunch of dead guys like Charles Wesley, Phillips Brooks, John Hopkins, Isaac Watts, and many more!

So many rich Christmas carols beautifully take us into the mission of Jesus. They connect the wooden[2] trough to the wooden cross; Mary's son to Mary's Savior; His magnificent birth to His maleficent death; His manger to His martyrdom; His annunciation to His atonement. Look to the hymns of Christmas and see the thread of redemption masterfully woven all throughout. The scarlet thread connects the cradle, the cross, and the crown. This is why, more than two thousand years removed from the event, we are still humbly astonished by His heavenly light.

Break forth, O beauteous heavenly light,
To herald our salvation;

He stoops to earth—the God of might,
Our hope and expectation.
He comes in human flesh to dwell,
our God with us, Immanuel,
The night of darkness ending,
Our fallen race befriending.[3]

What's Your Mission?

The very moment you became a follower of Jesus, your life's mission became inextricably bound to His. You no longer rule and reign over your own destiny; rather, His destiny defines you. So what was the mission of Jesus the Christ? We find it clearly communicated in His first recorded words, two penetrating questions that take us from the rugged trough all the way to the rugged cross.

Question 1: "Why did you seek Me?" (Luke 2:49). Why seek Jesus?

Question 2: "Did you not know that I must be about My Father's business?" (Luke 2:49). Why did Jesus come?

Get ready to encounter the Christmas Babe in a fresh new light! Let's hear from Him and witness the Light of life found in the first words of Jesus.

Come, Desire of nations, come!
Fix in us Thy humble home;
Rise, the woman's conquering Seed,
Bruise in us the serpent's head.
Adam's likeness now efface,
Stamp Thine image in its place;
Second Adam from above,
Reinstate us in Thy love.

"Hark! The Herald Angels Sing"

Let earth and heaven combine,
Angels and men agree,
To praise in songs divine
The incarnate Deity.

Charles Wesley
"Let Earth and Heaven Combine"

Gentle Mary laid her child lowly in a manger;
There He lay, the undefiled, to the world a stranger:
Such a babe in such a place, can He be the savior?
Ask the saved of all the race, who have found His favor.

Joseph Simpson Cook
"Gentle Mary Laid Her Child"

He came down to earth from heaven
Who is God and Lord of all,
And His shelter was a stable,
And His cradle was a stall:
With the poor, and mean, and lowly
Lived on earth our Savior holy.

C. F. Alexander
"Once in David's Royal City"

CHAPTER ONE

THE POWER
OF FIRST WORDS

The night was dark. The times were desperate. An oppressive government had called for a universal tax. A young teenage girl found herself in a "crisis" pregnancy. Under these dire conditions, just over two thousand years ago, the thought of "I'll Be Home for Christmas" was the furthest thing from the minds of Joseph and Mary as they journeyed to Bethlehem.

Well-advanced into pregnancy, Mary held tightly to the beast of burden as it nimbly stepped some eighty miles across all types of rugged terrain. Joseph no doubt contemplated many things on this perilous journey. Did he feel contempt toward Rome for its burdensome census? Was he replaying the angelic vision of his role in the Messiah's arrival?

Would they be attacked and robbed along the way? Where would they lodge once they arrived in the little town of Bethlehem? Were there rumors circulating about Mary's pregnancy and the true identity of the child's father? People could be so ruthless. Joseph easily could have put her away privately and moved on. Life would have been so much simpler for him without all of this drama.

Then, after all the exhausting travel, the young couple heard the discouraging words: *No room here.* Imagine this reception—or more accurately—*rejection* of the family about to usher in the King of kings. The innkeeper had no idea *whom* he was turning away. "He was in the world, and the world was made through Him, and the world did not know Him. He came to His own, and His own did not receive Him" (John 1:10–11).

"No occupancy" for the One who occupied heaven. No space for the eternal One who invaded our time and space, only to be left cribless. As the sacred hymn so aptly states,

> *Thou didst leave Thy throne and Thy kingly crown*
> *When Thou camest to earth for me;*
> *but in Bethlehem's home there was found no room*
> *for Thy holy nativity.*[1]

But there was room in the stable. Surely at this point the weary travelers longed for any place with a roof over it. And who in that little sleepy town knew that "the hinge of history is on the door of a Bethlehem stable."[2]

"Born in a Barn"

"What's the matter with you—were you born in a barn?" I still remember this expression, sarcastically hurled my way as a youth, for leaving the door open on a cold day. Yet there was no sarcasm surrounding the Lord's birthplace. We may glamorize the biblical account of His birth, but whether it was a cave or a barn, He was born in a place full of animals, feed, insects, straw, and other things that accompany livestock.

When God came down to earth, He came down in the humblest fashion. He came down in the roughest manner. And He came into a place of conflict, certainly not becoming of a king. Divinity invaded poverty. He traded His kingly robes for rough swaddling clothes. He traded His divine prerogatives for a humble feeding trough, the fragrance of royalty for the rough smells of livestock and manure. He spent His first night resting with the very animals He'd created. The Savior of the world was born in a place where many parents wouldn't even let their kids play out of fear of infection or injury.

> *Infant holy, Infant lowly, for His bed a cattle stall;*
> *Oxen lowing, little knowing Christ the babe is Lord of all.*[3]

Next time you're corrected for leaving the door open, you might want to winsomely reply, "Jesus was born in a barn. I'm following Him." Let's follow Him truly and hear from Him and His first powerful words.

First Words of Jesus

From the moment a child begins to mumble, many parents playfully dispute the child's first words. Did he say "daddy" or "mommy"? "Mimi" or "papa"? No doubt the debate ends at the 3 a.m. cry for food or a diaper change. There is power in the first words of a child, for words begin to unveil their personality, their likes and dislikes, and their passions. Parents long to hear the first words, because it begins a journey where their relationship with the child is deepened.

In the case of Jesus, Mary and Joseph would more likely have heard His first words in their small home in Egypt. Because of His divine nature, we know His first words were *not* "mine!" or "no!" We also know that it wasn't until Jesus was twelve that we would hear His first "recorded" words. In these words, as in all the words of the Bible, there is life-changing power.

The first recorded words of Jesus Christ, as God incarnated in human flesh, were, "Why did you seek Me? Did you not know that I must be about My Father's business?" (Luke 2:49). These two questions are the cornerstone of this book. In each chapter we'll journey through the Christmas narrative, tethering every event and character of Christmas to Jesus and His foundational first words. He is, after all, the essence of Christmas and life.

Naturally you may wonder, *I thought this was a Christmas book. What do the words of a twelve-year-old have to do with Christmas?* The answer: absolutely *everything*! Because these words encapsulate the very reason He was born in a manger that night divine. These first words unveil why Jesus Christ *is* the essence of Christmas and why He is so much more than just the nativity baby. They tell us volumes about the little stranger in the manger "whose goings forth are from of old, from everlasting" (Micah 5:2). Though the world traditionally celebrates His physical arrival into time and space on December 25th, these first recorded words reveal to us that this is God incarnate, the One who has no beginning and no end. (In fact, according to Colossians 1:16, the actual first recorded words of Jesus were "Let there be light" [Genesis 1:3].)

The power of His first recorded words as a young man reveal the passion and heart of the God-Man Jesus Christ. How appropriate that for Jesus, even at twelve years old, His words were all Daddy—all the time. Though He would love and respect Joseph, this was not about His earthly adopted father. This was all about God, His heavenly eternal Father. In the four Gospels, the "heaven-born Prince of Peace" addresses God as Father more than 160 times, including twice in His seven last words from the cross.[4]

From these first words, Jesus taught us that His relationship with His Father was the most important part of His existence, and thus it is the same for ours. He taught the disciples that because of Him, God was now their Father in heaven (Matthew 23:9). He taught them to serve their Father and even pray to their Father (Matthew 6:9). Although these are the only recorded words of Jesus in the three decades before He began His earthly ministry, He speaks from the beginning as a young man fully absorbed with the matters of His heavenly Father.

The Setting for His First Words

No one likes backtracking from a long journey—especially when you've forgotten something, or worse yet, *someone*! Most parents can identify with the horror of not knowing where their child is. Many a tear has been shed in the trauma and search for a missing little one. Wouldn't the worst-imaginable scenario be to lose Jesus Christ, the Son of God?

Mary and Joseph were leaving Jerusalem after their pilgrimage there for Passover. The Passover feast was an annual celebration, during which Jews from all over the world would come to Jerusalem to celebrate their exodus from Egypt (Exodus 12:1–14). Jesus was now older and truly the perfect son. They never had to worry about Him, until there was no sign of Him after the first day's journey home. In hurried desperation, Joseph and Mary frantically returned to the city and sought out their eldest son for three days. It wasn't inconceivable for a child, amid all the clamor and commotion of caravan travel, to get lost or left behind. Any parent would be driven crazy by the unanswered questions: "Where could He be?" "Didn't He hear the many calls to pack up and head out?" "Is He in some sort of trouble?" "Has He been hurt by robbers?"

Could this be the first time in His life that He had ever been disobedient?

Just twelve years earlier this same young couple had journeyed to the little town of Bethlehem, only five miles outside of Jerusalem. There they brought this child into the world. Now they had "lost" the very child born to "save the lost"—how ironic!

And Mary and Joseph probably asked themselves questions no other parent would even consider. These deeper questions most likely consumed their thoughts and conversation: "What about the angel and the prophecies?"; "Why are *we* on a search-and-rescue mission to find the One sent to rescue the world?"; "This doesn't seem to fit into the plan." Like the shepherds and the wise men, they were seeking Jesus, but in this case, to be reunited with Him. When they found Him, He was not in a store, a playground, or a game room, but in the temple of Almighty God.

> *Now so it was that after three days they found Him in the temple, sitting in the midst of the teachers, both listening to them and asking them questions. And all who heard Him were astonished at His understanding and answers. So when they saw Him, they were amazed; and His mother said to Him, "Son, why have You done this to us? Look, Your father and I have sought You anxiously."*
>
> Luke 2:46–48

Joseph and Mary found their son engaging some of the sharpest theological minds of the day and leaving them in awe. But still she would ask, "Son, why have You done this to us?" For a moment, Mary thought there was injustice and had taken Jesus's act as an affront. His response, however, would leave her breathless. "Why did you seek Me? Did you not know that I must be about My Father's business?" (Luke 2:49).

With just two questions, Jesus redirected his parents and called them to remember the purpose of His coming that night in the manger. He was here for His Father's business. In these words they hear the One who said, "Follow Me" ask them, "Why are you looking for Me?" What a curious question from the One sent to save a lost world. He wasn't disrupting their life; on the contrary, they were disrupting His. Quite a scene this must have been in the crowded temple. One could describe the setting as "when God came to church."

Though His parents were calling their son to leave Jerusalem with them, Jesus was summoned by another voice calling to Him, one of eternal familiarity. After all, He was in His Father's house hearing His Father's Word, surrounded by the sights and sounds of eternity. By now He well knew the fifth commandment and its adjoining blessing, "Honor your father and your mother, that your days may be long upon the land which the LORD your God is giving you" (Exodus 20:12).

The first recorded tension between His divine and human

nature is seen in this incident. "Veiled in flesh the Godhead see, hail the incarnate Deity, pleased as man with men to dwell, Jesus our Immanuel."[5] Yet here we see Him honor His heavenly Father and His earthly mother and stepfather perfectly. But in His Father's house, everything else was just background noise, meaningless chatter. At the feast of Passover, this young Passover Lamb was feasting on the all-satisfying sights and sounds of His Father. All other matters grew strangely dim in the light of God's domain. He was definitely in His element—enough to linger there for three days. All the older teachers of Israel around Him were moved to amazement. "And all who heard him were astonished at his understanding and answers" (Luke 2:47 KJV).

Mary's First Words to Jesus

In Mary's very first recorded words spoken to Jesus, she said, "Son, why have You done this to us? Look, Your father and I have sought You anxiously" (Luke 2:48).

The anxiety of His being missed was real. Real enough to bring a rare word of frustration aimed at the perfect child. This was the child who was never wrong. Mary and Joseph had divinely learned from the angel of their son's mission before He was born. Yet, in all the chaos of life, their mission had eclipsed His, and hence the conflict. The young family had already endured a lot of difficulty. The birth had been inconvenient. They had braved dangerous roads and trails in their long journey to Bethlehem only to find no room in the inn. Fleeing to Egypt, as refugees, to escape a murderous monarch had been difficult. Now they were back in Jerusalem, and He was twelve years old *going on eternity*. Their well-choreographed family trip to worship God at Passover had come completely unhinged. Surely, like all pious Hebrew families, they submitted their plans to God's will. His will, they would discover, was something far greater than anything they had conceived.

Try to savor the gravity and irony of this situation. At Passover, in the house of God, they found the perfect Lamb of God, the Word made flesh. They were too embroiled in their earthly prerogatives to understand His divine aspirations. Their mood was now different. The Christmas spirit from Bethlehem had dissipated. Like many throughout the ministry of Jesus and throughout the ages, they sought Him for the wrong reasons. They looked for Him in order to accomplish their mission. Simply put, they needed to get home. Jesus's mission was inconvenient to their itinerary. This wasn't supposed to happen! So, how did the Chosen One respond?

Two Life-Changing Questions

The answers to the two questions of Jesus is this book's driving force. His answers provide a divine link between the cradle and the cross that may forever change how you view Christmas, life, and eternity. Jesus Christ was purpose-driven. From all eternity He was on task, on mission, on point, and on purpose. What was this mission?

Jesus's response to His parents was divinely revealing in the following ways:

- He asked them questions and listened, just as He did a few verses earlier with the religious teachers (Luke 2:46).
- He answered their question with questions, just as He would do throughout His public ministry.
- He defined His mission in His questions.
- He answered perfectly and respectfully.
- He asked questions that struck awe in the religious teachers, His parents, and all those around Him.
- He uttered words that perfectly connected His birth to His ministry, to His death on the cross, and to His resurrection.

The Cradle and the Cross

Jesus's first words tie it all together. He tells us why He came and why we should seek Him. He declares in these words why we celebrate Christmas, Good Friday, and Easter. He discloses to us the essence of His nature and purpose. We have in His first words the grand revelation of a person who transcends any season or holiday. His words tie together all aspects of His life in perfect symmetry. Watch how His mission, as set forth in these first words, connect and contrast the cradle with the cross in the chart on the next page.

1. Roman law led to His traumatic birth in a cattle trough.	1. Roman law sentenced Him to His traumatic death on a wooden cross.
2. Born in Bethlehem, the city of bread.	2. The bread of life was broken at Golgotha.
3. The good news of the Gospel first came to the lowly shepherds.	3. The good news of the Gospel was last given to the lowly thief.
4. Mary's pain in childbirth.	4. Mary's pain in her child's death.
5. Marked by the brightness of a star at birth.	5. The morning star was covered in oppressive darkness at death.
6. Blessed by the giving of gifts from wise men.	6. Cursed by the taking of His clothes for gambling by fools.
7. The first cry of birth.	7. The last cry of death.
8. Accepted and embraced in love and care.	8. Rejected and forsaken in judgment and wrath.
9. Blessed and worshiped.	9. Cursed and mocked.
10. Born inside a stable and clothed.	10. Died outside in the open air and stripped of clothing.

Question One: Why Do You Seek Him?

Church attendance always skyrockets at Christmastime. Tragically, we all too often seek Christmas more than we seek Christ. Even those interested in the Christ of Christmas rarely want anything to do with the *cross* of the Christ of Christmas. "Give me the cuddly little baby on the golden bed of straw. Not the bloodied man dying on the tree of death." When the season is in full swing, multitudes gladly proclaim, "We love Christmas!" It's as though the holiday itself has become an idol to many. Very few hasten to proclaim, "We love Christ!"

So He simply asks: "Why are you seeking Me?" Madly rushing here and there, we can relate at some level to the anxiety of Mary and Joseph in their "seeking." We hustle, argue, fight, and "jingle a lot of bells." We plan and desperately strive for that "perfect" Christmas Day. Yet how often does the Lord Jesus Christ get preempted by our stress and busyness.

But Christmas, just like every day, is about seeking Jesus. It is not just about bending our knee to take a present from under the tree. It's about "Come adore on bended knee, Christ the Lord, the newborn King." In the following chapters, we'll meet the others who sought Jesus in the Christmas narrative: the shepherds, Mary and Joseph, Herod, Anna, Simeon, and the wise men. We'll discover *why* each of them looked for Him. We'll see how they all were uniquely connected to His mission.

So, why do *you* seek Him? Are you like the crowd of John 6, which clamored to Jesus for miracle bread but were repulsed by the thought of consuming the "Bread of Life"? Or are you like the blind man of John 9? At the call to follow Christ, he joyfully believed and worshiped Jesus. "Then he said, 'Lord, I believe!' And he worshiped Him" (John 9:38). He's more than a seasonal, candle lighting "Christmas fix." He is the eternally luminous fixture. Without Him we are doomed to eternal darkness. He is calling you to follow Him completely all year round. He doesn't just show up in the manger at the holidays to assuage your guilt for lack of church attendance the rest of the year. Nor does He merely appear at weddings and funerals—when the realities of life break upon you like crashing waves against the rocks.

He invaded time and space for a reason. It's found in the hymns and carols of the season. It's seen joyfully all around us, if we'll simply hear "heaven and nature sing." Splendid angels brought the first noel of His mission "to certain poor shepherds in fields as they lay." Wise men brought gifts that amplified His mission. Herod feigned worship, and then tried to murder Him before He could fulfill His mission.

Why do you seek Him?

Question Two: Do You Know the Mission of Jesus?

Brilliantly, Jesus answers His first question within another question: "Did you not know, that I must be about My Father's business?" Jesus had laser focus. The main thing was the main thing. Everything else was distracting noise. His Father's business was His mission above all else. The same mission is embedded in the Christmas carols we so often voice with little comprehension of their profound import. Lyrics like,

He comes to make His blessings flow,
*   far as the curse is found,*[6]

To save us all from Satan's power,
*   when we were gone astray,*[7]

Light and life to all He brings,
*   risen with healing in His wings,*
Mild He lay his glory by,
*   born that men no more may die,*
Born to raise the sons of earth,
*   born to give them second birth.*[8]

Unwittingly, Mary and Joseph stepped right in the middle of the Son of God's eternal mission statement. They were the ones who were *lost*. A defining moment indeed! Did they catch on? Did they get on board with His mission? Here's what Luke 2:50 tells us about their reaction: "But they did not understand the statement which He spoke to them."

Sadly, our world does not understand Jesus's mission. It did not then, and even today, many claiming to follow Jesus don't truly grasp His mission. But here is the answer of all answers. He was about accomplishing His earthly task, which began in the stable. It would take Him to the cross, for the glory of the Father and the salvation of the lost! The essence of His mission is the heart of the Gospel. He accomplished everything we couldn't, and He offers us everything we don't deserve.

Maybe you can identify with Mary and Joseph. Maybe you're not sure why Jesus came or why people even celebrate Christmas. But you know deep inside there is something infinitely important about all of this. You know there is power in His words, just as Mary knew. In fact, the very next verse tells us, Mary "treasured all these things in her heart" (Luke 2:51 NIV). Perhaps you do know the facts of His grand mission, but you've "cooled off" and become detached from the One sent to transform your life.

Ultimately the Christmas narrative is only a part of His larger mission as revealed in His first words. Connect with Jesus and His mission, and you will find the only true and lasting treasure of meaning and hope.

Come to Him and You Will Never Be the Same

In the next chapters we'll journey together to connect with Jesus Christ and His transforming mission. We'll discover how He can forever change our lives. We'll find out why He really is the Christmas gift that keeps on giving and giving and giving.

Are you ready for a new beginning? Just as His light filled

that dark, dirty stable on that holy night in Bethlehem, so He can come into the darkness of your life and fill it with His light. Maybe now is the time for you to humble your heart before Him and receive the ultimate gift of salvation. Simply respond to the first words of Jesus, which He spoke at the start of His public ministry.

"The time is fulfilled, and the kingdom of God is at hand. Repent, and believe in the gospel."

Mark 1:15

You can call upon Him now, by praying something like, "Dear heavenly Father, thank You for the gift of Your Son, the Lord Jesus Christ. I repent of my sin and admit my complete inability to meet the perfect demands of Your law. I believe the good news that Jesus died in my place and I humbly ask You to save me from my sin. I receive the gift of salvation and new life in Christ. Thank You for saving me and making me Your child. In Jesus's name, amen."

"O Holy Night" is one of the most well-known Christmas hymns—and one of my personal favorites. Did you know it was originally written in France in 1847 by backslidden poet/wine merchant Placide Cappeau de Roquermaure? He gave us a true treasure in this song. His words were then put to music by Jewish composer Adolphe Charles Adams. "O Holy Night" was the very first song ever played on the radio. Radio silence was broken on Christmas Eve 1906, when Reginald

Fessenden first read a portion of the advent scripture from Luke's Gospel. He then took up his violin and played this sacred hymn—and what a hit it has been![9]

Next time you hear "O Holy Night" over the airwaves, will it be just another song on your daily commute, or will these rich lyrics resonate with you? Has your soul felt its true worth?

> *Long lay the world in sin and error pining,*
> *till He appeared and the soul felt its worth.*
> *A thrill of hope the weary world rejoices*
> *for yonder breaks a new and glorious morn;*
> *fall on your knees, oh hear the angel voices.*
> *Oh night divine, oh night when Christ was born.*

SCRIPTURE REFLECTIONS
ON THE FIRST WORDS OF JESUS

"And your house and your kingdom shall be established forever before you. Your throne shall be established forever."

According to all these words and according to all this vision, so Nathan spoke to David.

2 Samuel 7:16–17

For unto us a Child is born,
Unto us a Son is given;
And the government will be upon His shoulder.
And His name will be called
Wonderful, Counselor, Mighty God,
Everlasting Father, Prince of Peace.

Isaiah 9:6

"But you, Bethlehem Ephrathah,
Though you are little among the thousands of Judah,
Yet out of you shall come forth to Me
The One to be Ruler in Israel,
Whose goings forth are from of old,
From everlasting."

Micah 5:2

"When Israel was a child, I loved him,
And out of Egypt I called My son."

Hosea 11:1

Then Joseph, being aroused from sleep, did as the angel of the
Lord commanded him and took to him his wife, and did not
know her till she had brought forth her firstborn Son. And he
called His name JESUS.

Matthew 1:24–25

Then He taught, saying to them, "Is it not written, 'My house
shall be called a house of prayer for all nations'? But you have
made it a 'den of thieves.'"

Mark 11:17

Then He went down with them and came to Nazareth, and was
subject to them, but His mother kept all these things in her heart.
And Jesus increased in wisdom and stature, and in favor with
God and men.

Luke 2:51–52

Then He said to them, "These are the words which I spoke to
you while I was still with you, that all things must be fulfilled
which were written in the Law of Moses and the Prophets and
the Psalms concerning Me."

Luke 24:44

Now the Passover of the Jews was at hand, and Jesus went up to Jerusalem.

John 2:13

And He said to those who sold doves, "Take these things away! Do not make My Father's house a house of merchandise!" Then His disciples remembered that it was written, "Zeal for Your house has eaten Me up."

John 2:16–17

Now before the Feast of the Passover, when Jesus knew that His hour had come that He should depart from this world to the Father, having loved His own who were in the world, He loved them to the end.

John 13:1

Therefore, just as through one man sin entered the world, and death through sin, and thus death spread to all men, because all sinned.

Romans 5:12

For if by the one man's offense death reigned through the one, much more those who receive abundance of grace and of the gift of righteousness will reign in life through the One, Jesus Christ.

Romans 5:17

Therefore purge out the old leaven, that you may be a new lump, since you truly are unleavened. For indeed Christ, our Passover, was sacrificed for us.

1 Corinthians 5:7

He who sins is of the devil, for the devil has sinned from the beginning. For this purpose the Son of God was manifested, that He might destroy the works of the devil.

1 John 3:8

GROUP DISCUSSION QUESTIONS

1. Why do we tend to glamorize the Christmas story?

2. What were your first words, and why are they significant?

3. Why was God's house so attractive to Jesus?

4. How could Mary and Joseph possibly lose Jesus?

5. Who was really lost when Jesus was at the temple?

6. What does the birth of Jesus have to do with His death?

7. Why do people seek Jesus at Christmas?

Now let us all with gladsome cheer
Go with the shepherds, and draw near
To see the wondrous gift of God,
Who hath His own dear Son bestowed.

Martin Luther
"From Heaven Above to Earth I Come"

"Fear not!" said he; for mighty dread
had seized their troubled mind,
"Glad tidings of great joy I bring
To you and all mankind."

Nahum Tate
"While Shepherds Watch Their Flocks"

Break forth, O beauteous heavenly light,
And usher in the morning;
Ye shepherds, shrink not with affright,
But hear the angel's warning.
This Child, now weak in infancy,
Our confidence and joy shall be.
The power of Satan breaking,
Our peace eternal making.

Johann von Rist, trans. John Troutbeck
"Break Forth, O Beauteous Light"

Herdsmen beheld these angels bright—
To them appeared with great light,
And said, "God's son is born this night."

"In Excelsis Gloria"

CHAPTER TWO

THE GREATEST MESSAGE TO THE LOWLIEST OF MESSENGERS

I s Christmas a pagan holiday or a Christian tradition?" The phone lines light up like a Christmas tree every December when I ask that one simple question on my national radio show. We get into discussions of calendars. Wasn't Jesus really born in the springtime? How much ritual paganism has been enmeshed in our Christian worship? While this makes for a great discussion and sizzling hot ratings, it becomes easy to miss the point of Jesus's birth. His birth is less about *when* and far more about *who* and *why*. In the midst of all the controversy, one fact is irrefutable.

Jesus Christ was born. God became a man and changed history. One of the most remarkable points of the whole Christmas story is to *whom* He first brought the message—

the shepherds. If you were to send out a very important announcement to some very important people about a very important person to be born, these characters would never make the list!

> While shepherds feared and trembled
> When lo! Above the earth
> Rang out the angel chorus
> That hailed our Savior's birth.[1]

No Jewish child ever dreamed of growing up to be a shepherd. These nomads were typically illiterate, uneducated, and outcasts. Considered the lowest rung on the societal ladder, their testimony wasn't even admissible in a Hebrew court of law. Because of their dealings with animals and Gentiles, and their working on the Sabbath, they were often deemed "unclean"—not even allowed to enter the temple. The expression "dumb as sheep" could likely be expanded to "dumb as shepherds."

In the world's eyes, such inarticulate men should be the *last* ones assigned to articulate the most profound message in history. No human writer could ever have scripted this providential display of 1 Corinthians 1:27: "But God has chosen the foolish things of the world to put to shame the wise, and God has chosen the weak things of the world to put to shame the things which are mighty."

Throughout history, some of the greatest Bible characters

were shepherds. Abel's lamb was the first acceptable sacrifice to God (Genesis 4:4). Abraham, Isaac, and Jacob all kept sheep. Moses herded sheep for forty years, then herded the people of Israel out of Egypt. Before he became Israel's greatest king, David spent years in obscurity caring for sheep. The prophet Amos was a shepherd as well. The role of the shepherd has always been near the heart of the Lord. Ultimately, all of these figures point to the Great Shepherd. "Now may the God of peace who brought up our Lord Jesus from the dead, that great Shepherd of the sheep, through the blood of the everlasting covenant, make you complete in every good work to do His will, working in you what is well pleasing in His sight, through Jesus Christ, to whom be glory forever and ever. Amen" (Hebrews 13:20–21).

The first Noel the angel did say
was to certain poor shepherds in fields as they lay.[2]

In a remote field, outside of the "little town of Bethlehem" on that first Christmas night some two thousand years ago, the greatest news came first to some of the very least in society. These nameless shepherds were sent to a tiny and seemingly insignificant nearby town.

Why Bethlehem? "Bethlehem (Hebrew: 'house of bread') is about five miles southwest of Jerusalem, in the fertile hill country of Judah, cradled between two ridges and located in the main highway from Jerusalem to Egypt. Its name came from the grain produced there in Old Testament times, and it is an especially fitting name for the place where the Bread of Life was born (John 6:35)."[3]

Just as Bethlehem was called "least" by the prophet Micah (Micah 5:2), so the shepherds were thought to be the "least." Decades before the Christmas child grew up and "preach[ed] good tidings to the poor" (Isaiah 61:1), God's mighty angel brought the Gospel to these poor lowly characters near this obscure little town. "And there were in the same country shepherds abiding in the field, keeping watch over their flock by night. And, lo, the angel of the Lord came upon them, and the glory of the Lord shone round about them, and they were sore afraid" (Luke 2:8–9 KJV).

> *While shepherds watched their flocks by night,*
> *   all seated on the ground,*
> *The angel of the Lord came down,*
> *   and glory shone around.*[4]

Suddenly, the poorest and least likely of candidates struck gold and received the best news in history. Of all the power players in the first century, why did the glorious news of the great Savior's birth first come to these outcasts? Not the royals, the rich or religious elite of the day, but common shepherds received the "good tidings of great joy." Their initial reaction was not one of great joy, but of great fear in the presence of God's glory.

Silent night, holy night,
shepherds quake at the sight.[5]

The Glory of God

"And the glory of the Lord shone around them" (Luke 2:9). God's glory lit up the night and paralyzed these men with fear. Their entire life flashed before their eyes. But they were about to begin a new life—a life of grand purpose, found in the child of promise. So what exactly is the glory of God?

John Piper states that it is near impossible to define the glory of God. His culminating definition is, "The glory of God is the infinite beauty and greatness of God's manifold perfections."[6] J. I. Packer further explains the following: "Glory means Deity in manifestation. . . . Wherever we see God in action, there we see His glory—He presents Himself before us as holy and adorable, summoning us to bow down and worship."[7]

The glory of God is declared by His creation. "The heavens declare the glory of God" (Psalm 19:1). The same glory of God appeared to Abraham, Isaac, and Jacob. His glory shone in a burning bush to Moses. The prophets of old, such as Ezekiel and Isaiah, were overwhelmed by the presence of God's glory (Ezekiel 1:28; Isaiah 6:1–3). Then that first Christmas night, His radiant glory engulfed these humble shepherds. We see this throughout the scriptures as God's glory:

- Appeared in Creation—Genesis 1:1–9; Psalm 19:1

- Appeared to patriarchs—Genesis 18:13–16
- Appeared to Moses—Exodus 3:2; Exodus 33:18–23
- Appeared to Israel—Exodus 13:21–22
- Appeared in the tabernacle—Exodus 40:34–38
- Appeared in the temple—2 Chronicles 7:1-3
- Appeared to the Prophets—Isaiah 6:1–8; Ezekiel 1:28

Four hundred years of darkness and silence passed by in what's historically known as the "intertestamental period." There was no word of revelation from God, His prophets, or His glory between Malachi and Matthew. Then suddenly the glory of God appeared in full brilliance to these shepherds. Once they experienced God's glory, His peace and goodness would fill them, just as the angel declared. Notice how the *inward* response to God's *upward* glory produced *inner* peace. How? They were about to connect with the glory of God in the face of Jesus Christ (2 Corinthians 3:18).

On an obscure hillside surrounded by wooly animals, the shepherds came face-to-face with the luminous splendor of the glory of God. In the blinking of an eye, they went from counting sheep to encountering an angelic choir. "Glory to God in the highest, And on earth peace, goodwill toward men!" (Luke 2:14). A more literal translation of this verse is "Peace on earth with whom God is well pleased." This doesn't mean there was sudden peace on earth universally, but peace to those who believe in the Prince of Peace.

"And the Word became flesh and dwelt among us, and

we beheld His glory, the glory as of the only begotten of the Father, full of grace and truth" (John 1:14). The same glory that sent them to the ground in the field, sent them to their knees in the stable, where they beheld the Lord of glory.

> *Sing choirs of angels, sing in exaltation,*
> *O sing, all ye bright hosts of heaven above.*
> *Glory to God, all glory in the highest!*[18]

First Words of the Angels to the Shepherds

From that moment on, they would never be the same. "And the angel said unto them, Fear not: for, behold, I bring you good tidings of great joy, which shall be to all people. For unto you is born this day in the city of David a Saviour, which is Christ the Lord" (Luke 2:10–11 KJV).

"Fear not" were the first words. This heavenly host was not dispatched to inflict fear but to proclaim good news. This was "good tidings of great joy." The very same great joy of God's peace and presence would also later impact the wise men. There's something spectacular about this good news that dispenses joy to the hearers. We find the answer in the angel's description of the babe. He pronounces the three seminal titles of Savior (which means deliverer), Christ (anointed one, or messiah), and Lord (sovereign master, also used in the Old Testament as a name for God).

Picking themselves up off the ground, the humble herdsmen go from near death to new life. They go to see the One who would save them, who would become their anointed one, and their God. The glory of God delivers them from meaningless obscurity and sends them straight to Jesus, their King. The Father's business is about to become their business.

> *Flocks were sleeping, shepherds keeping*
> *Vigil till the morning new*
> *Saw the glory heard the story,*
> *Tidings of a gospel true.*
> *Then rejoicing free from sorrow,*
> *Praises voicing greet the morrow;*
> *Christ the babe is born for you,*
> *Christ the babe was born for you.*[9]

The Sign

"You will find the Babe wrapped in swaddling cloths, lying in a manger" (Luke 2:12). Of all the grand signs Creator God could give, why the manger? Shepherds were no strangers to mangers. Caring for animals was their livelihood. The angels' sign fit these first responders perfectly. They lived and breathed in the world of smelly stalls, stables, and mangers. Their very own animals might have eaten from the same trough they sought this Christmas night. Except this manger would hold the source of all life Himself.

Certainly they were well acquainted with the setting and scents of a stable, but definitely not one occupied by the Lord of Glory. A "king-sized" bed indeed! What a wondrous thought: those sinful, rough, bedraggled shepherds humbly bowing before the Lamb of God who takes away the sin of the world. They had nothing to offer Him but their hearts. On that silent night in the least likely place, the least-worthy people encountered the "Savior, which is Christ the Lord." Their lives became the first fulfillment of the angels' words. Joy to the world first came to the world's cast-offs, the lowly shepherds.

First Words of the Shepherds

Shepherds in the fields abiding,
watching o'er your flocks by night
God with man is now residing,
yonder shines the infant light.[10]

After being bewildered and bedazzled by the heavenly host, the shepherds' first words appear on the pages of scripture. "So it was, when the angels had gone away from them into heaven, that the shepherds said to one another, 'Let us now go to Bethlehem and see this thing that has come to pass, which the Lord has made known to us'" (Luke 2:15).

"Let us now go"—the shepherds were immediately drawn into a brand-new mission. A remarkable unity, like no other, suddenly possessed them. God's glory is contagious, creating here a powerful bond of "let us." In their first words we have the first statement of "let us" in the New Testament. Hebrews 10:22–24 presents us with three of these poignant expressions—*let us* draw near, *let us* hold fast, and *let us* consider one another. Theologians commonly refer to this as the three heads of "let us" in the scripture. Have you experienced the joy of the Gospel in community with others?

The shepherds demonstrate tremendous unity of purpose. *Let us* is not "individual," but "flock" language. "Let us now go to Bethlehem and see" now defines them as a band of brothers on a new mission that will transform them from shepherds to sheep. In addition to their new mission, they took action and responded to God's revealed word, "which the Lord has made known to us." Suddenly, they were in a hurry, and "came with haste," to encounter the glory of God bundled up in the baby Jesus. The angels went back to heaven, and these third-shift workers wasted no time. They responded immediately to pursue the living Christ.

Christmastime can be divisive and tense. So many people call my talk show at Christmastime to share painful stories of disunity. Many times it involves people who claim Christ as their Lord and Savior. How tragic that while believers fight amongst themselves, the world continues to live in darkness, desperate for His light. These shepherds never took a class on "unity in the body of Christ," but we can learn volumes from their example.

The enemy wants to divide and isolate believers into loneliness and blame. But Christ came to set the captives free and to unite us (John 17:21). He brings us into His grand mission of bringing His glory to our lost world in need of the

Gospel. The mission of the Savior unified them and changed their lives forever!

Changed by Jesus Christ

> *Who is He in yonder stall*
>> *At whose feet the shepherds fall? . . .*
> *'Tis the Lord! O wondrous story!*
>> *'Tis the Lord! the King of glory.*[11]

The transformation of the lives of these men bookends the gospel account of the Christmas narrative. Luke 2:8 tells us, "And there were in the same country shepherds abiding in the field, keeping watch over their flock by night" (KJV). Exactly what were they doing that holy night? Telling empty tales filled with idle chatter? Sharing off-color jokes? Or perhaps they were bemoaning their pointless lives? Just a few verses later in Luke 2:20 we read: "And the shepherds returned, glorifying and praising God for all the things that they had heard and seen" (KJV).

So what happened between these two verses in the nativity narrative to transform ordinary, obscure shepherds into some of the first evangelists? Though God was in the manger, God was also at work. The Friend of sinners was about to transform His first visitors. There may have been "no room at the inn" but there was room in the stable to accommodate these first guests. Their hearts were gladly filled with the One they encountered.

His work began in them as they first saw the glory of God light up their dark world. Then, they made haste to go and see God in the city of David, Israel's legendary shepherd-king. Likely David tended sheep in these same fields where he penned the words "The LORD is my shepherd" (Psalm 23). Like sheep gone astray (Isaiah 53:6), they left their flock, not to be lost, but to be found. Though shepherds, in a moment, they became sheep. They followed the Great Shepherd and King of kings, the offspring of Israel's shepherd-king David, in the city of David.

Next, Luke tells us that they spread the good news widely to the marvel of everyone (Luke 2:20). Something supernatural happened to these societal outcasts to turn them into divine ambassadors, the first missionaries of Jesus Christ. Before Jesus uttered His first words in the temple, the shepherds were fully committed to His mission.

Isn't this the essence of Christmas? Isn't this the reason Jesus came down? God's amazing goodness and grace poured out to the least likely and the undeserving. The light of the Morning Star penetrates the darkest of hearts. Would not the babe in the Bethlehem manger grow up to teach: "Blessed are the poor in spirit," "blessed are the meek," and "the least will be the greatest" (Matthew 5:3, 5; Luke 9:48)? Did not the Friend of sinners say, "I have not come to call the righteous, but sinners" and "unless . . . you become as little children, you will by no means enter the kingdom of heaven" (Matthew 9:13; 18:3)"?

"The least" were first on the scene at Jesus's birth. In His earthly ministry, "the least" were part of His greatest mission all the way to the cross:

- The lowly shepherds
- The rough, uneducated fisherman for disciples
- The tax collectors and sinners
- The poor
- The lepers, lame, blind, and deaf
- The Samaritans
- The Gentiles
- The lowly thief

The shepherds didn't miss the real meaning of Christmas, because the Christ of Christmas was "everything" to them! They went from "abiding in their fields" to "abiding in Christ," from "keeping watch over their sheep" to "responding to the good news of the Great Shepherd." They truly experienced "Peace on earth and mercy mild, God and sinners reconciled."

Illiterate and with no theological training, Jesus's first missionaries were changed by His glory. What happens next in the shepherds' lives powerfully displays what happens when anyone experiences His glory. Upward, outward glory translates into deep inner peace. "Heaven came down and glory filled their soul."[12] When they found Jesus, they found peace and a whole new purpose—His mission. The gift of Christmas wasn't a nicely wrapped package under a well-lit tree. No, it was the God-child bundled in a feeding trough in a dimly lit stable.

Today we're so inculcated in our materialistic culture that, like the Bethlehem inn, our lives are too crowded for Christ. We have so much that there's no room left for Jesus—the only One who can meet our deepest needs. But when the glory of Christ came to the lowly shepherds, unlike the innkeeper, they had plenty of room for His life to fill theirs. The empty would become filled, and the humble would be exalted. The meek would inherit the earth. And it didn't stop there. They didn't selfishly keep it to themselves, but they spread the good news everywhere. Their life took on a whole new meaning, because of the *life* they encountered in the stable. Proclaiming the wondrous news of life would now become their mission.

> *Shepherds, why this jubilee?*
> *Why your joyous strains prolong?*
> *What the gladsome tidings be*
> *Which inspire your heavenly song.*[13]

The Cross

Just like salvation came to the lowly shepherds in the first hours of Jesus's life, so salvation came to the lowly thief in the last hours of Jesus's life. This beautiful gift of salvation can't fill a vessel already brimming with self and pride. Salvation only comes to the humble. "God resists the proud, but gives grace to the humble" (James 4:6). The shepherds *first* heard the good news of the Savior, Christ the Lord—at His birth. The thief *last* heard the blessing of the good news from the Savior's lips—at His death. Of all the people at the scene of the cross, why does Jesus pardon this thief? Why not one of the religious elite, military leaders, or wealthy merchants passing by? He poured out His grace to the least qualified and the least likely. The only one granted eternal life at the scene of cross was the treacherous thief. Though he was high and lifted up on his own tree of death, his heart was humble and bowed low before the Lord of glory, and he cried, "Lord, remember me when You come into Your kingdom" (Luke 23:42). To which Jesus replied, "Assuredly, I say to you, today you will be with Me in Paradise" (Luke 23:43).

The Good Shepherd poured out His life ministering to despised tax collectors, the poor, sick, needy, outcast, and condemned criminals. "I have not come to call the righteous, but sinners, to repentance" (Luke 5:32 KJV).

It's widely believed that due to the proximity to Bethlehem and Jerusalem, the sheep there were likely raised for temple sacrifice. Even though they themselves were looked down on and considered outcasts, the *job* of these shepherds was quite important to the spiritual welfare of the people of Israel. For instance, Exodus 12:5 tells us that the Passover lamb must be male, first-born, and without spot or blemish. But while the shepherds tended their sheep, the perfect Passover Lamb was born in a nearby stable.

Who could begin to count the number of sheep raised for sacrifice throughout Hebrew tradition? Every year, thousands of gallons of blood would flow like a river out of the temple through the ancient aqueduct system, displaying the need for atonement. Generations of shepherds would have raised thousands of sheep to be slaughtered. Their death was a sign pointing toward the one perfect Lamb, who would eternally atone for sin.

The one the shepherds found in the manger, Mary's little lamb, was the only Lamb that could save them and "take away the sin of the world" (John 1:29).

> *Not all the blood of beasts on Jewish altars slain*
> *Could give the guilty conscious peace or wash away the stain.*
>
> *But Christ, the heavenly lamb, takes all our sins away*
> *The sacrifice of nobler name and richer blood than they.*
>
> *On Christmas day, God's Lamb was born that he might die.*
> *At Crucifixion time he died that we might live on high.*
>
> *Thus, life and death in him were joined in mystery.*
> *His life brought death, his death brought life to us eternally.*[14]

Let us humbly take a knee next to the shepherds at the cradle. Let us kneel beside the thief at the cross. May we there behold the Lord of glory and trust Him as our all-satisfying

Savior. Is there room in your heart for the only One who can fill it with forgiveness, healing, and peace? Or are you stuck on the 100-mph performance treadmill of life, futilely trying to earn His favor? Don't miss the gift of salvation that could only be earned by Jesus Christ, for He was the One who went from a cattle trough to Calvary's cross to pay the price for man's redemption. He was always about His Father's business!

Joy will abound and life will find true meaning when "every heart prepares Him room." Encounter Him and you will never be the same.

On Christmas Eve in 1865, Philadelphia pastor Phillips Brooks rode around the outskirts of Bethlehem on horseback. He had been commissioned to write a children's Christmas carol for his church. It was there, close to the shepherds and the actual birthplace of the Lord, that he found his inspiration. "O Little Town of Bethlehem" has become one of the greatest Christmas hymns of all time.[15] Like so many other sacred songs, Brooks's carol presents the historical Jesus and calls "meek hearts" to receive Him individually and personally.

May our hearts long to sing with the hymnist, "O holy child of Bethlehem, descend to us we pray. Cast out our sin and enter in. Be born in us today. We hear the Christmas angels, the great glad tidings tell. O come to us, abide with us, our Lord Emmanuel."

SCRIPTURE REFLECTIONS
ON THE FIRST WORDS OF JESUS

All we like sheep have gone astray;
We have turned, every one, to his own way;
And the LORD has laid on Him
the iniquity of us all.
He was oppressed and He was afflicted,
Yet He opened not His mouth;
He was led as a lamb to the slaughter,
And as a sheep before its shearers is silent,
So He opened not His mouth.

Isaiah 53:6–7

For thus says the High and Lofty One
Who inhabits eternity, whose name is Holy:
"I dwell in the high and holy place,
With him who has a contrite and humble spirit,
To revive the spirit of the humble,
And to revive the heart of the contrite ones."

Isaiah 57:15

"The Spirit of the Lord GOD is upon Me,
Because the LORD has anointed Me
To preach good tidings to the poor;
He has sent Me to heal the brokenhearted,

To proclaim liberty to the captives,
And the opening of the prison to those who are bound."

Isaiah 61:1

"But on this one will I look:
On him who is poor and of a contrite spirit,
And who trembles at My word."

Isaiah 66:2

Now it happened, as He was dining in Levi's house, that many tax collectors and sinners also sat together with Jesus and His disciples; for there were many, and they followed Him.

Mark 2:15

"I am the good shepherd. The good shepherd gives His life for the sheep."

John 10:11

But we all, with unveiled face, beholding as in a mirror the glory of the Lord, are being transformed into the same image from glory to glory, just as by the Spirit of the Lord.

2 Corinthians 3:18

Not with the blood of goats and calves, but with His own blood He entered the Most Holy Place once for all, having obtained eternal redemption.

Hebrews 9:12

And every priest stands ministering daily and offering repeatedly the same sacrifices, which can never take away sins. But this Man, after He had offered one sacrifice for sins forever, sat down at the right hand of God.

Hebrews 10:11–12

Now may the God of peace who brought up our Lord Jesus from the dead, that great Shepherd of the sheep, through the blood of the everlasting covenant.

Hebrews 13:20

And when the Chief Shepherd appears, you will receive the crown of glory that does not fade away.

1 Peter 5:4

GROUP DISCUSSION QUESTIONS

1. What would be a modern-day equivalent to a shepherd?

2. Why did good news of the Savior's birth first come to the lowly shepherds?

3. How would you describe the glory of God?

4. Where else do we find shepherds in the plan of God?

5. Why were the shepherds' lives changed?

6. What happened that brought them into sudden unity?

7. Is anyone beyond the saving reach of God's grace?

The One she carried in her womb would one day
carry her cross and come out of the tomb.

Stu Epperson

What child is this, who, laid to rest,
On Mary's lap is sleeping?
Whom angels greet with anthems sweet,
While shepherds watch are keeping?

William C. Dix
"What Child Is This"

To you this night is born a child
Of Mary, chosen virgin mild;
This little child, of lowly birth,
Shall be the joy of all the earth.

Martin Luther
"From Heaven Above to Earth I Come"

Christ, by highest heaven adored;
Christ the everlasting Lord;
Late in time behold Him come,
Offspring of the virgin's womb.

Charles Wesley
"Hark! The Herald Angels Sing"

The hand that rocked His cradle
rocked the babe who would rule the world.

Stu Epperson

CHAPTER THREE

HAVE A MERRY, MARY CHRISTMAS

M erry Christmas" is the phrase we long to say as the weather gets colder and December 25th draws nearer. Indeed, the celebration of the birth of the Lord Jesus Christ should be "merry" and joyful. After all, He came to pay the ransom for lost souls and entered the world to bring us eternal life. That is something to be *merry* about.

But the origin of the word "merry" was not in the most joyful of situations. In 1534 Bishop John Fisher was condemned to death by Henry VIII for not recognizing the king as the Supreme Head of the Church of England. As he was imprisoned in the Tower of London, he sent a message to Thomas Cromwell, the chief minister to Henry VIII, and said, "And this our Lord God send you a merry Christmas, and a comfortable, to your heart's desire."

Despite its dire beginning, the phrase slowly began to

be used more frequently in the coming centuries. In the sixteenth century, the hymn "God Rest Ye Merry, Gentlemen" began to be sung in churches throughout the world, making the term more notable.

"God Rest Ye Merry, Gentlemen" is the first time we find the reference in a Christmas song. When this tune was introduced more than five hundred years ago, the word "merry" meant great and mighty. In fact, in the Middle Ages, Robin Hood's men were "merry" men because they were strong and courageous. Thus, in its original meaning it encourages us to have a Christmas of strength and valor.[1]

God rest ye merry, gentlemen
Let nothing you dismay
Remember Christ our savior
Was born on Christmas day
To save us all from Satan's power
When we were gone astray
Oh tidings of comfort and joy, comfort and joy;
Oh tidings of comfort and joy.

The first part of the first verse tells us what a "merry" Christmas looks like. The rest of the first stanza and the chorus give us profound insight into the true meaning of a "merry Christmas"—His amazing hope and deliverance, "when we were gone astray."

It was not until 1843, when Charles Dickens wrote *A*

Christmas Carol, that the word received worldwide prominence. Dickens used it twenty-one times in the novel. In that same year the first commercially available Christmas card displayed the words "Merry Christmas." Today we find them on everything from lights on the front lawn to inflatable Santas. Though some can take this phrase today to mean something light and fluffy, when it was initially used it meant something entirely different.

Others have commonly used the phrase "Merry Christmas" as synonymous with the flow of wine and spirits celebrating the most wonderful time of year. The phrase has been diluted by our hedonistic world in many ways. A deeper search into the heart of God leads us to a greater encounter of TRUE merriment. When we say "Merry Christmas," the divine joy we feel truly is the same joy that was felt at Mary's Christmas.

Born of Mary, to Make Men Merry

A merry Christmas is not possible without the Mary of Christmas. Besides the baby Jesus Himself, no one commands more attention at Christmastime than His mother, Mary. Her remarkable journey as the vessel that brought "joy to the world" is the topic of many Christmas messages and sacred hymns. "Round yon virgin mother and child" dominates the Christmas narrative and the story of advent, the arrival of God's Son into the world of humankind.

But have you ever wondered what Mary experienced?

What was it like to give *birth* to the One who would give the *new birth* of salvation to a lost world?

Of all the vessels God could have used to bring His Son into the world, He chose a young, poor, unknown teenage girl. Before the Savior would carry the cross and be laid in the tomb, she would carry Him in her humble womb. Mary would carry the only child who had the power to make *her* a child of God and carry her to heaven.

But Mary was merry despite the difficult circumstances of His birth. She experienced firsthand the humility of the stable as the smell of cattle dung loomed in the air. Placing the King of kings in a manger encrusted with the saliva of livestock would not sadden her, but make her merry, for God was with her. Her deepest joy was before her. The child's mission would become her mission, and the world would never be the same.

She fed the One who would feed the five thousand. He who floated safely in her belly would one day walk on stormy waters. She dressed the One who would clothe her in righteousness. She bundled His tiny hands and feet long before they were pierced with nails of iron. She cuddled His tender side years before it would be thrust through with a Roman spear. Before the whip, the stripes, or the blows, His teeny smooth back she caressed. Christmas was more real to Mary than it was for any other human. One day she would stand at the foot of His cross, knowing He hung there to make them eternally merry.

First Words of Mary

It is only in the gospel accounts of Matthew and Luke that we encounter Mary before the birth of Jesus. Luke gives us Mary's entire genealogy from her great ancestor Abraham down through the legendary King David and beyond. We first hear from Mary in Luke 1, where the angel Gabriel, who previously appeared in the temple to Zacharias, now appeared to her:

> *Now in the sixth month the angel Gabriel was sent by God to a city of Galilee named Nazareth, to a virgin betrothed to a man whose name was Joseph, of the house of David. The virgin's name was Mary. And having come in, the angel said to her, "Rejoice, highly favored one, the Lord is with you; blessed are you among women!" But when she saw him, she was troubled at his saying, and considered what manner of greeting this was. Then the angel said to her, "Do not be afraid, Mary, for you have found favor with God. And behold, you will conceive in your womb and bring forth a Son, and shall call His name JESUS. He will be great, and will be called the Son of the Highest; and the Lord God will give Him the throne of His father David. And He will reign over the house of Jacob forever, and of His kingdom there will be no end." Then Mary said to the angel, "How can this be, since I do not know a man?"*
>
> Luke 1:26–34

These first words of Mary do not display doubt but faith. Surely her young mind was swirling with thoughts of her betrothal to Joseph. She obviously understood "where babies come from" and how this could quickly go bad for her with talk of scandal in the community. What would people say? Her family and friends would be shocked! At least her cousin Elizabeth, in her remarkable pregnancy, had a husband involved. Elizabeth even had the biblical precedent of God providing children to older, infertile mothers, such as Sarah, Abraham's wife, in Genesis 18. But in all of human history there had *never* been, nor would there ever be again, another virgin birth. This miraculous birth was no secret. It had been promised centuries before by the prophet Isaiah. The renowned words of Isaiah would have been acutely familiar to young Jewish girls: "Therefore the Lord Himself will give you a sign: Behold, the virgin shall conceive and bear a Son, and shall call His name Immanuel" (Isaiah 7:14). From when she was knee high, Mary, like the other Hebrew girls, might have dreamed of being God's chosen vessel for the Messiah.

With this in mind, Mary desired to know how the supernatural would invade the natural. Out of youthful innocence and sincere faith she inquired, "How can this be since I do not know a man?" Mary was eager to know how the Lord would move. On the surface, one could easily question Mary's motive as being doubtful, just as with Zacharias a few verses earlier in the chapter: "And Zacharias said to the angel, 'How shall I know this? For I am an old man, and my wife is well advanced in years'" (Luke 1:18).

Mary's first words display the depth of her faith. Zacharias demonstrated his doubt by asking for a sign to confirm what this angel declared. He was actually corrected by the angel for his response: "And the angel answered and said to him, 'I am Gabriel, who stands in the presence of God, and was sent to speak to you and bring you these glad tidings. But behold, you will be mute and not able to speak until the day these things take place, because you did not believe my words which will be fulfilled in their own time'" (Luke 1:19–20).

The holy angel answered Mary's question. There was no rebuke given, but understanding. "And the angel answered and said to her, 'The Holy Spirit will come upon you, and the power of the Highest will overshadow you; therefore, also, that Holy One who is to be born will be called the Son of God. Now indeed, Elizabeth your relative has also conceived a son in her old age; and this is now the sixth month for her who was called barren. For with God nothing will be impossible.' Then Mary said, 'Behold the maidservant of the Lord! Let it be to me according to your word.' And the angel departed from her" (Luke 1:35–38).

Before her divine son was supernaturally conceived, Mary became part of His mission. She was passionate about His Father's business. Mary wanted to know the plan, was given the plan, and was willing to live out the plan, for she believed the word of the Lord. The angel Gabriel saw the innocent inquiry in the young maiden's heart as opposed to the seeds of doubt in the older, trained theologian. Here are some fascinating comparisons and contrasts in these two people.

Comparing Mary and Zacharias

- Both were gripped by fear at the appearance of Gabriel.
- Both were immediately comforted with the words "fear not."
- Both received the good news of the impossible.
- Both encountered supernatural revelation.
- Both would be forever changed.
- Both would experience the fulfillment of Old Testament prophecies.
- Both would experience the fulfillment of the angel's words.
- Both heard a word from God after four hundred years of silence.

Contrasting Mary and Zacharias

- Zacharias was an old man/Mary was a young teenager.
- Zacharias was a seasoned priest of God/Mary was a young follower of God.
- Zacharias was married/Mary was single but betrothed.

- Zacharias doubted/Mary believed.
- Zacharias was admonished/Mary was praised.

While theologians may analyze and argue in favor or against the motives of Zacharias, we need only listen to the angel Gabriel. He had it right. The one who stood in the presence of almighty God praised the faith of Mary and punished the disbelief of Zacharias. Ironically, Zacharias's name means "Yahweh remembers." His wife Elizabeth's name means "covenant." Their son John's name means "grace." In one verse, Luke 1:72, the entire family's role is described: "To perform the mercy [John] promised to our fathers and to remember [Zacharias] His holy covenant [Elizabeth]." Yahweh remembered His covenant and gave them grace. Like so many of us who stumble, the humbled priest would go on to be used mightily and return to faith in God's promises. Zacharias's son, John the Baptist, would grow up to be the mighty forerunner of his cousin Jesus. He would later cry out, "Behold! The Lamb of God who takes away the sin of the world!" (John 1:29).

In the priest's experience with the angel, he was literally dumbstruck, verbally unable to patch things up. Mary, on the other hand, replied: "'Behold the maidservant of the Lord! Let it be to me according to your word.' And the angel departed from her" (Luke 1:38).

When confronted with God's word and calling, she responded in submission, as the Lord's "maidservant." Before

Paul, James, Jude, and other great authors of scripture identified themselves as "bondservants" of the Lord, there was young Mary, the "maidservant" of the Lord. For Mary was merry to serve.

Shortly after she submitted to the word of God, the "living" Word of God would be conceived inside the favored one of God. The seed of almighty God would be implanted in this young woman of faith. Her child would go on to change the world for all eternity.

Born of Mary, Born of God

In the fullness of time (Galatians 4:4), the plan that began in the garden was now set in motion. Mary was a glad participant in fulfilling the very first prophecy of Scripture, when God declared in Genesis 3:15, "And I will put enmity between you and the woman, and between your seed and her Seed; He shall bruise your head, and you shall bruise His heel." The seed of the woman was divinely conceived by the Holy Spirit in the virgin Mary. The Great King Eternal would be born as a lowly baby. The conqueror of sin, Satan, and death would ultimately crush the head of the serpent under His feet (1 John 3:8).

How could this be? Because Jesus Christ, though born in the vessel of Mary, was born of the seed of God the Father. The virgin birth is one of the most remarkable miracles in all of history. The Heidelberg Catechism sums it up like this: "That the eternal Son of God, who is and remains true and eternal God, took to himself, through the working of the Holy Spirit, from the flesh and blood of the virgin Mary, a truly human nature so that he might also become David's true descendant, like his brothers and sisters in every way except for sin."[2] Theologian J. I. Packer describes this grand mystery with these words: "It's here at the first Christmas, that the profoundest and most unfathomable depths of the Christian revelation lie. 'The Word was made flesh' (John 1:14); God became man; the divine Son became a Jew; the Almighty appeared on Earth as a helpless human baby, unable to do more than lie and stare and wriggle and make noises, needing to be fed and changed and taught to talk like any other child. Nothing in fiction is so fantastic as is this truth of the incarnation."[3]

In Mary we have the only human being to be a dual vessel of Christ. She carried Him to term and followed Him in time. Mary gave birth to Jesus physically and would one day herself experience new birth in Jesus, spiritually. One might go so far as to argue that she was twice chosen: once for the Messiah to be born of her, and a second time for her to be born of God (John 3:3). What an experience it must have been for Mary, to be the only person present at both the cradle and the cross.

Once in royal David's city stood a lowly cattle shed
Where a mother laid her Baby in a manger for His bed;
Mary was that mother mild, Jesus Christ her little Child.[4]

Mary Did Know!

What exactly did Mary know before that silent night, before she became "yon virgin mother and child"? How aware was she of God's plan before the arrival of the "holy infant so tender and mild"? Two key things indicate that Mary knew a lot more than we give her credit for. First, the angel gave her explicit revelation of what would happen to her (Luke 1:26–38). Second, we see it in her prayerful response. You can tell the depth of one's faith by the depth of one's prayer life. In Luke 1 we get a glimpse into one of the most beautiful prayers in the Holy Scriptures, widely known as Mary's *Magnificat*.

> *"My soul magnifies the Lord,*
> *And my spirit has rejoiced in God my Savior.*
> *For He has regarded the lowly state of His maidservant;*
> *For behold, henceforth all generations will call me blessed.*
> *For He who is mighty has done great things for me,*
> *And holy is His name.*
> *And His mercy is on those who fear Him*
> *From generation to generation.*
> *He has shown strength with His arm;*
> *He has scattered the proud in the imagination of their*
>   *hearts.*
> *He has put down the mighty from their thrones,*
> *And exalted the lowly.*
> *He has filled the hungry with good things,*
> *And the rich He has sent away empty.*

He has helped His servant Israel,
In remembrance of His mercy,
As He spoke to our fathers,
To Abraham and to his seed forever."

Luke 1:46–55

"My soul magnifies the Lord." From this phrase we derive the prayer's name, *Magnificat,* which in Latin magnifies the greatness of God as "an utterance of praise." It is clear from this opening line that Mary has a high view of God. She also has a high view of God's Word, since practically all of the words of this prayer are right out of Scripture. Her ancestor David said in Psalm 34:3: "Oh, magnify the LORD with me, and let us exalt His name together."

"My spirit has rejoiced in God my Savior." A proper view of God is always accompanied by the realization of our utter need for His deliverance. How profound that the mother of the Savior is here worshiping God as Savior. In 1 Samuel 2:1, we hear the voice of another young maiden, by the name of Hannah, magnifying her Savior for a son she knew only God could give. "My heart rejoices in the LORD; my horn is exalted in the LORD. I smile at my enemies, because I rejoice in Your salvation."

We know Mary was God-centered. Her prayer was God-centered. Her life orbited around the mission of God. Before she carried the living Word of God in her womb, she treasured the written Word of God in her heart (Psalm 119:11). His truth informed her life. Mary was a woman of the Word even before the Living Word of God was conceived in her. A closer study of Mary's words, prayers, and actions clearly demonstrates her spiritual maturity. Look at how the Scriptures tell us of Mary's awareness of her special son:

- Luke 2:19: "But Mary kept all these things and pondered them in her heart."
- Luke 2:33: "And Joseph and His mother marveled at those things which were spoken of Him."
- Luke 2:51: "But His mother kept all these things in her heart."

Take a moment to meditate on the profound words of this divinely inspired prayer. Notice the rich reflections of Gods amazing attributes and actions. Witness a prayer fully centered on "hallowed be Thy name" and a life fully trusting God's will and mission. Picture yourself praying Mary's prayer. This is a true prayer of Christmas, because there is no Christmas without Christ the Savior.

Mary's Mission

Mary's mission was to serve in the greater mission of Jesus, the mission that Christ would be born in lost sinners to make them new. Just as the miracle of the virgin birth goes against all biological and scientific laws, so also does the miracle of new birth. The birth of Jesus is possible only by God's infinite power. Likewise, new birth in Jesus is only possible by God's miraculous power. Even the astute Jewish leader Nicodemus was perplexed by this concept when he came to Jesus one night, as recorded in John 3. When Jesus declared to him, "Unless one is born again, he cannot see the kingdom of God" (John 3:3), Nicodemus asked, "How can a man be born when he is old? Can he enter a second time into his mother's womb and be born?" (John 3:4).

As the Holy Spirit of God conceived Jesus in Mary, so the new birth takes place by the Spirit's conception (John 3:5; Romans 8:9). Just as Christ supernaturally inhabited the womb of the humble servant Mary, so likewise He only inhabits hearts that humbly believe on Him. Both conceptions and births are supernatural and defy human explanation. Matthew 19:26 tells us that the only way anyone can be saved is with God, the only One who can work the impossible. Both involve an incorruptible seed: "Having been born again, not of corruptible seed but incorruptible, through the word of God which lives and abides forever" (1 Peter 1:23).

Both the birth of Christ in history and the sinner's new birth in Christ only happen by God's power—purely of divine prerogative and origin. "But as many as received Him, to them He gave the right to become children of God, to those who believe in His name: who were born, not of blood, nor of the will of the flesh, nor of the will of man, but of God" (John 1:12–13).

Though I grew up in a strong Christian home, as a young child, I was quite confused about *how* exactly to get Jesus inside of me. I had always heard the expression "Ask Jesus into your heart," but I wasn't exactly sure of its meaning. No, the phrase doesn't appear in the Bible; and yes, it's widely misunderstood. Yet many parents use it as a simple description to convey to their children the idea of receiving Christ as their indwelling Lord.

A friend of mine, Pastor J. D. Greear, actually wrote a book entitled *Stop Asking Jesus into Your Heart: How to Know for Sure You Are Saved*. His goal wasn't to start a "theological riot" but rather to dispel unhealthy myths about salvation and to clearly proclaim the Gospel. J. D. describes belief in these terms: "Belief is the hand that lays hold of the finished work of Christ. . . . Faith's sole object is the finished work of Christ." He goes on to say, "Paul's words to the Philippian jailer were simple and sufficient, 'Believe on the Lord Jesus Christ and you shall be saved.' Believing in the Lord Jesus Christ means acknowledging, submissively, that Christ is the Lord and that He accomplished our salvation, just as He said He did—and resting our hopes there."[5]

Believing in Jesus is essential to being saved by Him as Paul also says in Romans, "If you confess with your mouth the Lord Jesus and believe in your heart that God has raised Him from the dead, you will be saved." When you fully believe and trust Him and only Him for your salvation, you are miraculously placed in Christ.

When singing "Emmanuel" at Christmas, we must never

forget that "God with us" means we can be "in Him" because of the good news of great joy in the gospel of Jesus Christ. That's why He came "for poor ornery sinners like you and like I."[6]

Colossians 1:27 declares the indwelling Christ: "To them God willed to make known what are the riches of the glory of this mystery among the Gentiles: which is Christ in you, the hope of glory." Every time I read these words, I am in awe of God's glorious work to place Himself in me to change me. There is no greater merriment than the glory He has given us in Christ.

Never again will Jesus physically occupy a human being as He did Mary. But, yes, Jesus will spiritually occupy the life of a newborn believer by the power of the indwelling Holy Spirit (1 Corinthians 6:19). "The Word was made flesh and dwelt among us" (John 1:14 KJV). He brings the wonderful news of salvation to our fallen world. It is His Word that convicts the sinner. His Spirit supernaturally transforms the heart into a new creation. Jesus was about His Father's business as the living Word of God. He "fulfilled all righteousness" in His perfect life. He was the perfect sacrifice in His death. He rose from the dead in victory. Now He calls sinners by His life-changing Word to believe and be made new. "Therefore, if anyone is in Christ, he is a new creation; old things have passed away; behold, all things have become new" (2 Corinthians 5:17).

By His grace the sorrow of death is gone and the merry of life is forevermore. Because Christ was born of Mary at Christmas, we can merrily sing, "O come, thou Dayspring, come and cheer our spirits by Thine advent here; disperse the gloomy clouds of night, and death's dark shadows put to flight. Rejoice! Rejoice! Emmanuel shall come to thee, O Israel!"[7]

Mary at the Cross

At His death on the cross, Jesus cared for the woman who had cared for Him at His birth. He dispatched the disciple John to look after Mary as her adoptive son. "When Jesus therefore saw His mother, and the disciple whom He loved standing by, He said to His mother, 'Woman, behold your son!' Then He said to the disciple, 'Behold your mother!' And from that hour that disciple took her to his own home" (John 19:26–27). Mary's pain in bringing forth her firstborn son in a cattle trough in no way compared to the agony of soul she felt at the foot of His cross. No mother should endure the anguish of watching her own son die, and in such a horrible fashion. She experienced unthinkable anguish as she watched her son, the "everlasting light," hang in the darkness. Yes, "a sword was piercing her soul," just as the older man Simeon had prophesied in the temple when Jesus was dedicated as a baby. Mary, whose name means "bitter," well identified with the bitter depth of pain at the cross of Christ.

Mary, beneath the cross, surrounded by love
A reflection of how things had been
She heard the Savior's first cry
Compassion now cries out to her.[8]

The mission that began in the manger was now being completed at the cross. Mary uniquely experienced two births. The birth in the stable and the new birth in her soul had beautiful similarities. She brought forth her firstborn son in the pain of birth. He would painfully die in her place to bring her forth into salvation's new birth. She delivered the One who would deliver her. Just as the Holy Spirit conceived Jesus in her physical body, the same Spirit of God saved her. Profound indeed! The thought of Jesus Christ indwelling someone physically! Yet this is the miracle of the virgin conception and birth. By the angel's own admission the virgin birth is regarded as impossible. Impossible by human standards but not God's: "for with God nothing will be impossible" (Luke 1:37).

The words "It is finished" (John 19:30) rang out triumphantly. Among those hearing those words firsthand was Mary, the mother of Jesus. In this moment, Mary's little lamb was both the Lamb of God "who takes away the sins of the world" (John 1:29) and the Good Shepherd laying His life down for His sheep (John 10:11). Mary's bitterness would become eternally sweet.

Crown Him the virgin's Son,
The God Incarnate born
Whose arm those crimson trophies won
Which now his brow adorn;
Fruit of the mystic rose,
As of that rose the stem;
The root whence mercy ever flows,
The Babe of Bethlehem.[9]

When He ascended to the Father, He sent us the Holy Spirit of God to seal and indwell every one of His followers as the family of God. Though Mary was His mother, if you have received the Son, she is your sister. For Christ was in her, to be born for her, and for lost sinners to be reborn. Her merriment at the good news of the angel and her merriment at the birth of her Son revealed her humble heart of faith. Mary received the double blessing of caring for Jesus *and* receiving Him as her Savior. That is a merry, Mary Christmas.

SCRIPTURE REFLECTIONS
ON THE FIRST WORDS OF JESUS

"And I will put enmity
Between you and the woman,
And between your seed and her Seed;
He shall bruise your head,
And you shall bruise His heel."

Genesis 3:15

And a multitude was sitting around Him; and they said to Him,
"Look, Your mother and Your brothers are outside seeking You."
But He answered them, saying, "Who is My mother, or My
brothers?" And He looked around in a circle at those who sat
about Him, and said, "Here are My mother and My brothers!
For whoever does the will of God is My brother and My sister
and mother."

Mark 3:32–35

"Is this not the carpenter, the Son of Mary, and brother of James,
Joses, Judas, and Simon? And are not His sisters here with us?"
So they were offended at Him.
But Jesus said to them, "A prophet is not without honor ex-
cept in his own country, among his own relatives, and in his own
house."

Mark 6:3–4

And they were greatly astonished, saying among themselves, "Who then can be saved?"

But Jesus looked at them and said, "With men it is impossible, but not with God; for with God all things are possible."

Mark 10:26–27

Jesus answered and said to him, "Most assuredly, I say to you, unless one is born again, he cannot see the kingdom of God."

John 3:3

Now there stood by the cross of Jesus His mother, and His mother's sister, Mary the wife of Clopas, and Mary Magdalene.

John 19:25

When Jesus therefore saw His mother, and the disciple whom He loved standing by, He said to His mother, "Woman, behold your son!" Then He said to the disciple, "Behold your mother!" And from that hour that disciple took her to his own home.

John 19:26–27

But when the fullness of the time had come, God sent forth His Son, born of a woman, born under the law, to redeem those who were under the law, that we might receive the adoption as sons.

Galatians 4:4–5

GROUP DISCUSSION QUESTIONS

1. What do you mean when you say, "Merry Christmas"?

2. How much did Mary know about the One she carried in her womb?

3. How did the birth of Jesus change the lives of Joseph and Mary?

4. What about Mary's mission connected her to the mission of Jesus?

5. How was she a "dual vessel" of the Lord?

6. How would you describe the similarities between the virgin birth and the new birth of salvation?

7. What does it mean to be born again?

Child in the manger, Infant of Mary,
Outcast and stranger, Lord of all;
Child Who inherits all our transgressions,
All our demerits on Him fall.

Mary M. Macdonald, trans. Lachlan Macbean
"Child in the Manger"

And in despair I bowed my head:
"There is no peace on earth," I said,
"For hate is strong, and mocks the song
Of peace on earth, good will to men."

Henry W. Longfellow
"I Heard the Bells on Christmas Day"

Yet with the woes of sin and strife
the world has suffered long;
Beneath the angel strain have rolled
two-thousand years of wrong;
And man, at war with man,
hears not the love-song which they bring;
O hush the noise, ye men of strife,
and hear the angels sing.

Edmund H. Sears
"It Came upon the Midnight Clear"

CHAPTER FOUR

THE DARK SIDE OF CHRISTMAS

"A voice was heard in Ramah,
Lamentation, weeping, and great mourning,
Rachel weeping for her children,
Refusing to be comforted,
Because they are no more."

Matthew 2:18

It's the most wonderful time of the year" may be piping out of our radios, but truth be told, in our hearts we often sing, "It's the most depressing time of the year."

But why? Why so much pain at Christmastime? No other time of year amplifies the pain of the human heart than this season. Families will gather without parents, sons, or daughters, who were taken way too early in life. Many families won't gather at all because of the painful rifts and feuds dividing them. What about a family who has lost their son? How do you greet a friend at Christmas whose wife just died of cancer? What about the many families torn apart by divorce, separation, or imprisonment? And what does this have to do with the mission of Jesus Christ?

The Darkest Day of Christmas

Could you imagine the ghastly thought of mass funerals for small children at Christmastime? Not long after the birth of Jesus, this was a gruesome reality. Every story has a villain, but few compare to the one we'll meet in this part of the Christmas story. No one wants to think of Christmas as a time of bloodshed and gore. It would seem unthinkable to associate Christmastime with the barbaric murder of a town's entire population of young boys. Unfortunately, this is no tall tale, but a tragic reality perpetrated by Herod the Great. Herod provides a graphic and very real symbol of the pain experienced by so many at the holidays. Just as those Bethlehem families had *no* "merry little Christmas" in Jesus's day, so multitudes today suffer greatly this time of year.

Herod was an accomplished builder who erected fabulous structures across Israel. Among his works were the greatest additions to the temple in Jerusalem since the days of King Solomon. Yet, while attempting to make an architectural heaven on earth, Herod the Great created hell on earth. He left a ruthless trail of blood everywhere he went.

Egocentric, ambitious, and power-hungry, Herod murdered his own sons to prevent their succession. Consumed by insecure jealousy and suspicion, he even had his mother-in-law murdered. King Herod was not Jewish but an Edomite, a descendent of Esau. Similar to his ancestor Esau, Herod's life was marked by bitterness and all kinds of trouble (Hebrews 12:15–16). Just before his death he rounded up many of the respected families in the community. In his own twisted way, he ordered all of them to be executed at the exact time of his passing—so the whole country would mourn at his death. Still, no pain in life can be compared to the death of one's child, and Herod gladly inflicted such pain on a large scale. He does his darkest evil here, when Jesus was just an infant.

First Words of Herod the Great

How ironic that Gentile (non-Jewish) eastern religious leaders known as magi first brought word of the prophesied king to Herod. "Now when Jesus was born in Bethlehem of Judaea in the days of Herod the king, behold, there came wise men from the east to Jerusalem, saying, Where is he that is born King of the Jews? For we have seen his star in the east, and are come to worship him" (Matthew 2:1–2).

Scriptures record that Herod was upset when news of another Jewish king reached his ears. "When Herod the king had heard these things, he was troubled, and all Jerusalem with him" (Matthew 2:3). It's been said, "When Herod coughed, all of Jerusalem caught a cold." The people were troubled along with him. They knew this could mean pain or even death based on his degenerate history. So troubled was Herod, that he suddenly found religion. He became one of the first in a long line of celebrities to get excited about Christ and Christmas. He would certainly make his mark as the most notorious, nefarious Christmas celebrity ever. Just like Jesus's parents did in Luke 2:45, Herod looked for Jesus, but for the *worst* of reasons—to destroy Him. This politician didn't want to *kiss* a baby, he wanted to *kill* one.

In order to eliminate Christ, he had to find Him, and where better to go for answers than church? "And when he had gathered all the chief priests and scribes of the people together, he inquired of them where the Christ was to be born" (Matthew 2:4). Herod sought out the religious authorities to find Jesus. In fact, it's possible he consulted the same religious leaders who would hear the first words of Jesus just about a decade later.

Indeed, Mary and Joseph also sought out Jesus and found Him among the religious leaders. Both the wicked king, at Jesus's infancy, and the young parents found themselves confronted with His mission to the contradiction of their own agenda. "Now so it was that after three days they found Him in the temple, sitting in the midst of the teachers, both listening to them and asking them questions" (Luke 2:46).

Both Herod and Jesus's parents (ten years later) searched for Him among the brightest minds in Jerusalem. Both King Herod and young King Jesus (a few years later) asked questions of Jewish scholars. King Herod would use this information to inflict death on many, while King Jesus would willingly suffer death to save many souls. Shortly after his inquiry, King Herod would die empty and pass into a Christless eternity. Nearly two decades after young King Jesus's inquiry, He would suffer and die to eternally save sinners. King Herod will bow to the One he so viciously sought to kill (Philippians 2:10).

Listen to these seemingly pious words of this savage king: "And he sent them to Bethlehem and said, 'Go and search carefully for the young Child, and when you have found Him, bring back word to me, that I may come and worship Him also'" (Matthew 2:8). Just as during election season in America, when candidates suddenly find religion, King Herod knew how to play the part. On the surface his statement sounds super-spiritual. In fact, someone could surely generate a lot of positive response on social media by posting a verse like Matthew 2:8. However, a closer look at this verse will reveal some troubling issues.

Herod was *only* five miles away from the Messiah, but unwilling to take the trip. He delegated the seeking of Jesus to others. Though his own motives were depraved, the Bible is clear on seeking God. It must be done directly (Jeremiah 29:13). Herod also said one thing with the objective of doing the exact opposite. Herod would say anything to destroy another possible contender to the throne. He used everyone in his life as a pawn to advance his murderous ambitions.

The magi wisely heeded the angel's warning and traveled home another way. Once Herod pinpointed the Savior's birthplace, however, he rained down wholesale execution on all males age two and under. "Then Herod, when he saw that he was deceived by the wise men, was exceedingly angry; and he sent forth and put to death all the male children who were in Bethlehem and in all its districts, from two years old and under, according to the time which he had determined from the wise men" (Matthew 2:16).

Can you imagine what it must have been like for the little town of Bethlehem, and its surrounding districts, devastated by all of this bloodshed? How horrendous is the thought of young mothers having their sons ripped from their arms and savagely slain by Herod's soldiers. Mourning all over town for precious young children doesn't seem compatible with "'Tis the season to be jolly." Such suffering certainly proves to be antithetical to the nativity narrative. So why is this in the Bible? Why does it ever happen? Why the Holocaust? Why the killing fields of Cambodia? Why have so many died in bloody wars? Why all the victims of ruthless terrorism? And why have so many little ones been taken so suddenly?

William Chatterton Dix was only in his twenties when he wrote "What Child Is This?" and "As with Gladness Men of Old" in 1859. The son of a successful surgeon, young William had been expected to go into medicine just like his father. Instead he sold insurance and wrote poetry. It was during a prolonged illness and a severe bout with depression one

Christmas that William Dix wrote these famous carols. The inspiration came when the pain of his life intersected with the pain of the cross. His understanding of the Christ baby's mission to the cross became well pronounced in his lyrics, especially in this rarely sung stanza of "What Child Is This?"

Why lies He in such mean estate,
here ox and ass are feeding?
Good Christians, fear, for sinners here
the silent Word is pleading.
Nails, spear shall pierce Him through,
the cross be borne for me, for you.
Hail, hail the Word made flesh,
The Babe, the Son of Mary.

One of my heroes of the faith, Joni Eareckson Tada, has experienced the supernatural grace of the cross of Christ through decades of being confined to a wheelchair. As a result of a tragic diving accident as a teenager, Joni became a quadriplegic. Yet in her deepest pain, she met Christ and His cross. From her "rolling pulpit," the Lord has used her ministry to impact millions over the years. When I mentioned this book to her, she told me about a painting that she created several years ago. It has the mother Mary cuddling baby Jesus with a cross in the backdrop. She graciously agreed to let me use it as an illustration. Here are her encouraging insights on Dix's classic carol, "What Child Is This?": "We are amazed that God the Son would become a man, but equally astounding is that a man or woman can become a son or daughter of God. The nativity is a holy story, but also *human*."[1]

The One Who Feels Your Pain

The answer to our pain comes in the form of the lone survivor of Herod's genocide, the Christ child. He was spared their brutal fate that day, according to the gospel of Matthew: "Now when they had departed, behold, an angel of the Lord appeared to Joseph in a dream, saying, 'Arise, take the young Child and His mother, flee to Egypt, and stay there until I bring you word; for Herod will seek the young Child to destroy Him.' When he arose, he took the young Child and His mother by night and departed for Egypt" (Matthew 2:13–14).

Jesus would one day bear the full weight of the victims' pain, and that of their families, and that of the world. On the cross Jesus would experience the deep pain of *every* parent's loss—combined—all bound together in infinite suffering. Ultimately, there at Golgotha He endured the judgment and wrath of God and took the punishment that was due lost sinners. Three hours of darkness marked the most painful moments in history, and the words He cried were "My God, my God, why hast thou forsaken me?" (Matthew 27:46 KJV; Mark 15:34 KJV).

Yes, at the darkest moment in all of history Jesus asked, "Why?" And in this why question we see *why* we are in such desperate need of a Savior. Jesus came in the humility of a cattle trough to ultimately suffer the humiliation of a Roman cross—to seek and save the lost (Luke 19:10). This was the heart of His mission. In spite of the pain, the torment, the evil, and the burden, He *never* backed down. No despot, tyrant, or ruler could ever inflict the pain endured by the Son of God on the cross. The trail of blood from Herod's Bethlehem massacre would ultimately flow to the place of the skull outside Jerusalem. There Jesus was "wounded for our transgressions, He was bruised for our iniquities; the chastisement for our peace was upon Him, and by His stripes we are healed" (Isaiah 53:5).

Nor could any other human being experience that level of pain. We may say "I feel your pain," but in reality we can't, simply because everyone's pain is different. Jesus *alone can* and *does* feel your pain. "Surely He has borne our griefs and carried our sorrows" (Isaiah 53:4). Miraculously, the Savior experienced unfathomable pain—all piled on Him at the cross. Pain is ultimately the result of our sin and a fallen world: "Therefore, just as through one man sin entered the world, and death through sin, and thus death spread to all men, because all sinned" (Romans 5:12).

Jesus's Pain, Our Gain

Repeatedly, the book of Hebrews tells us to *consider Him*. It says, "For consider Him who endured such hostility from sinners against Himself" (Hebrews 12:3). He is the One who was despised and rejected by men, a man of sorrows and acquainted with grief (Isaiah 53:3). The truth of Christmas is that Jesus came into a world of pain. The innkeeper rejected Him at His birth; He endured the pain of hostility all the way to the cross. He invites you now with His pain-scarred hands and feet to receive the gift of His life.

Taking "the Cross" Out of Christmas

The Christmas season brings with it the annual Christmas cultural battles. I have done many talk shows and heard many sermons on the subject of "Taking the Christ Out of Christmas." Whether it's the "political correctness" of the next retailer gone rogue or yet another government school that censors a harmless nativity scene, it's everywhere.

But have you ever considered that it's not the *baby* Jesus but the *cross* of Jesus that's so offensive? Most people aren't offended by the Christ of the cradle. Even the most secular among us can tolerate the cute little infant in the manger. In fact, it's become a huge part of our holiday merchandising mania. Retailers may gladly display a nativity scene outside their storefront in order to make the cash register "ring in the holidays." But start talking about the cross and you've got big trouble! Paul said it well in 1 Corinthians 1:23: "But we preach Christ crucified, to the Jews a stumbling block and to the Greeks foolishness." While many Christmas celebrations are quite inclusive of baby Jesus, they're expressly exclusive of baby Jesus's mission.

Give me the cradle not the cross
Adore Him as baby, not as Boss.
Bring His gifts for my fill,
His presents to ease my load.
Don't bid me surrender to Him my will,
nor travel down Calvary's narrow road.[2]

Where there is no cross, there can be no Christmas. There is no gain of a Savior without the pain of the Savior. There can be no "gift" of life in the cradle without the "giving" of His life on the cross. Jesus came to die, so we could live. He was born to die so we could be reborn and saved from eternal death—to live with Him forever.

We find the gift *wrapped* in the cradle. We see the gift divinely *opened* and shared at the cross. Alive from the tomb, the Giver of all life is crowned at His victorious resurrection. Consider the glorious contrast of all these dimensions. Joyous light and celebration accompanied His birth. Utter darkness and forsakenness enveloped Him at death. He supremely reigns in glory and honor in His resurrection and return—crowned King Eternal. Cradle, cross, and crown—all bundled up in one glorious being: the Lord Jesus Christ Himself.

Born Thy people to deliver,
Born a child, and yet a King,
Born to reign in us forever,
Now Thy gracious Kingdom bring.

By Thine own eternal Spirit,
Rule in all our hearts alone;
By Thine all-sufficient merit,
Raise us to Thy glorious throne.[3]

Only Jesus can lighten your burden and light up your life. "In Him was life, and the life was the light of men" (John 1:4). We don't hear about the star anymore after the wise men, because the Morning Star has come. King Herod, along with all the forces of evil, have come "to steal, and to kill, and to destroy." King Jesus says, "I have come that [you] may have life, and . . . have it more abundantly" (John 10:10).

This was His Father's business. He invaded the darkness of a lost and broken world. Will you allow Him into the dark corridors of your brokenness? There's nothing too painful or broken in your life that His light can't heal. That's why He went from the cradle to the cross, to vanquish the pain inflicted by all the evil "Herods" in history and to bring light into our darkness.

The King of kings lay thus in lonely manger;
In all our trials born to be our friend.
He knows our need; our weakness is no stranger.[4]

Will you let the Light of the world into your darkness? Will you allow Him to heal your deepest pain?

SCRIPTURE REFLECTIONS
ON THE FIRST WORDS OF JESUS

A good name is better than precious ointment,
And the day of death than the day of one's birth;
Better to go to the house of mourning
Than to go to the house of feasting,
For that is the end of all men;
And the living will take it to heart.

Ecclesiastes 7:1–2

Surely He has borne our griefs
And carried our sorrows;
Yet we esteemed Him stricken,
Smitten by God, and afflicted.
But He was wounded for our transgressions,
He was bruised for our iniquities;
The chastisement for our peace was upon Him,
And by His stripes we are healed.
All we like sheep have gone astray;
We have turned, every one, to his own way;
And the LORD has laid on Him the iniquity of us all.

Isaiah 53:4–6

"Behold, we are going up to Jerusalem, and the Son of Man will be betrayed to the chief priests and to the scribes; and they will condemn Him to death and deliver Him to the Gentiles; and they will mock Him, and scourge Him, and spit on Him, and kill Him. And the third day He will rise again."

Mark 10:33–34

And being in agony, He prayed more earnestly. Then His sweat became like great drops of blood falling down to the ground.

Luke 22:44

For Christ also suffered once for sins, the just for the unjust, that He might bring us to God, being put to death in the flesh but made alive by the Spirit.

1 Peter 3:18

And I heard a loud voice from heaven saying, "Behold, the tabernacle of God is with men, and He will dwell with them, and they shall be His people. God Himself will be with them and be their God. And God will wipe away every tear from their eyes; there shall be no more death, nor sorrow, nor crying. There shall be no more pain, for the former things have passed away."

Revelation 21:3–4

GROUP DISCUSSION QUESTIONS

1. Why is Christmas one of the hardest times of the year?

2. How would you describe the pain felt in Bethlehem after Herod's massacre?

3. How could Herod's words be so good, yet his actions be so evil?

4. Why is Jesus the only One who feels your pain?

5. How does that change things eternally?

6. Why is it so important to put the cross back in Christmas?

7. How can His light meet you in your darkest places?

He has opened heaven's door, and man is blessed forevermore.
Christ was born for this! Christ was born for this!

Heinrich Suso, trans. John M. Neale
"Good Christian Men Rejoice"

As they offered gifts most rare at that manger rude and bare;
So may we with holy joy, pure and free from sins alloy,
All our costliest treasures bring,
Christ, to Thee, our heavenly King.

William C. Dix
"As With Gladness Men of Old"

This Flower, whose fragrance tender with sweetness fills the air,
Dispels with glorious splendor the darkness everywhere;
True man, yet very God, from sin and death
He saves us, and lightens every load.

Friedrich Layritz, trans. Harriet Reynolds Krauth
"Lo, How a Rose E're Blooming"

O come, Thou Wisdom from on high,
And order all things, far and nigh;
To us the path of knowledge show,
And cause us in her ways to go.

trans. John M. Neale
"O Come, O Come, Emmanuel"

This gift of God we'll cherish well,
That ever joy our hearts shall fill.

trans. Theodore Baker
"How Great Our Joy!"

CHAPTER FIVE

THE WISEST CHRISTMAS SHOPPERS

We three kings of orient are,
bearing gifts we traverse afar. . . .

If you went Christmas shopping to buy a present for Jesus Christ, what would you get Him? What earthly gift could ever be fit for heaven's child? We all use the worn-out cliché: "What do you get someone who has everything?" *Only* in the case of the Christ child is this absolutely true! Because He is the Gift of God (John 3:16), the Giver of Life (John 1:4), and in Him "are hidden all the treasures of wisdom and knowledge" (Colossians 2:3). The star brought the wise men to the One who not only has everything, but who spoke everything into existence.

But who were they, and why did they seek Jesus? And whatever could wise men from afar give to the "wisdom" of the ages?

First Words of the Wise Men

"Now after Jesus was born in Bethlehem of Judea in the days of Herod the king, behold, wise men from the East came to Jerusalem, saying, 'Where is He who has been born King of the Jews? For we have seen His star in the East and have come to worship Him'" (Matthew 2:1–2).

From my earliest childhood years, I've always been fascinated with the story of the wise men and their gift selections. We don't know exactly how many wise men there were—though tradition claims there were three of them to go with the number of gifts. We don't know precisely where they came from—though many claim that *the East* is a reference to Persia. It's also believed they were influenced by the prophet Daniel and the Hebrew Scriptures: "Then the king promoted Daniel and gave him many great gifts; and he made him ruler over the whole province of Babylon, and chief administrator over all the wise men of Babylon" (Daniel 2:48). We don't know if in fact they were kings—though some historians have referred to them as "kingmakers." We do know they were "wise men," also known as magi (μάγοι *magi,* a wise man or astrologer). Most likely these were wealthy, knowledgeable, powerful, and influential men. To gain an audience with King Herod, they had to be persons of substance.

To say they were "star-struck" would be an understatement. These ancient scholars had laboriously studied the prophets and signs—and were probably impacted by the writings of the prophet Daniel. In their lives, they had no doubt amassed wealth, wisdom, power, and success. Yet something far deeper was missing. The answer came from something, or even, *Someone* who was the *only* One who could satisfy the hungry soul. The only thing that mattered to them was finding the Son. So they searched far and wide at great cost of time and fortune. Finally, these noblemen ended up in the holy city of Jerusalem, the closest coordinate to their last star spotting. Their agenda was simple—to find Jesus and fall down before the tiny King in worship. Worship was at the heart of their mission. We see this clearly in their posture, their passion, and their presents.

Like the shepherds before them, and His parents later on, they searched for Jesus. Apparently their lifelong search for everything else didn't fully satisfy. In complete contrast to the lowly shepherds, the well-to-do wise men had it all. So why go looking for more? The shepherds only had sheep, while the wise men used animals to carry their wealth. The shepherds barely existed, impoverished and empty—ready to be filled. The wise men had been so filled with wealth and power that the deepest needs of their souls were lacking. With minds and purses full, yet spirits empty, the wise men might well have heeded the second stanza of "Angels from the Realms of Glory."

> *Sages leave your contemplations,*
> *Brighter visions beam afar;*
> *Seek the great desire of nations,*

Ye have seen His natal star:
Come and worship, come and worship,
Worship Christ the newborn King.[1]

Notice the remarkable differences between the wise men and the shepherds:

Wise Men	Shepherds
1. Wealthy	1. Poor
2. Well-educated	2. Uneducated
3. Successful	3. Ordinary
4. Powerful	4. Insignificant
5. Influential	5. Unknown
6. Noble	6. Common
7. Cultured	7. Unpolished
8. On the move	8. Local
9. Long-time seekers	9. New seekers
10. Foreign	10. Native
11. Gentiles	11. Jews

The Mystery of the Star

For centuries, much discussion, debate, and conjecture has revolved around the "Beautiful Star of Bethlehem." We really know very little. One thing we do know is that the wise men were wise indeed when it came to stars and astronomy. They were the high-level scholars of their time. As elite scientists, these men were likely sought out by many for their wisdom and guidance. Since there were no star apps or advanced tele-scopes in those days, they devoted much of their life to the observation, study of, and possibly even worship of celestial lights. In ancient times heavenly luminaries influenced agri-culture, travel, time, calendar, and seasons. For certain, when the wise men first observed this supernatural star, they knew something was different, something grand enough to leave everything behind on a quest for the chosen king.

Notice that they called the star, "His" star. Something was even more remarkable about the star that connected it with Him specifically. Some theologians assert that the star was the "shekinah glory" of Israel—the very glory of God. The same resplendent glory that enshrouded Mount Sinai in Exodus 33. The same glory that dwelt in the most holy place of the Hebrew tabernacle and eventual temple. Because we see so much of God's glory resting upon the God-child, could this be the same glory of God as "the Word of the Father now in flesh appearing"? John 1:14 states, "And the Word became flesh and dwelt among us, and we beheld His glory, the glory as of the only begotten of the Father, full of grace and truth." Later in the Garden of Gethsemane, Jesus prayed, "And now, O Father, glorify Me together with Yourself, with the glory which I had with You before the world was" (John 17:5).

According to God's plan, the Light of the world was born at night. The radiant brightness of God's star penetrated the darkness. Furthermore, nothing incites worship like the glory of God. "Shepherds quaked" when the "glory of the Lord shone round about them." The magi claimed that their express purpose was to "worship Him." But what was it about this particular light in the sky that caused these men of substance to sojourn over "hill and fountain, moor and mountain, following yonder star"? They witnessed the glory of God! That same glory seen by the shepherds confronted these sages from afar.

Since the last star sighting was closest to the holy city, that was where they went. They marched their entourage into the Jewish capital of Jerusalem, announcing their intentions directly to nefarious King Herod. For all they knew, it was Herod's son they were seeking. Not a chance. They would soon learn that the two things you never utter in the presence of an egomaniacal sovereign were "worship" and "King of the Jews."

God's Word clearly revealed where Jesus was to be born.

But you, Bethlehem Ephrathah,
Though you are little among the thousands of Judah,
Yet out of you shall come forth to Me
The One to be Ruler in Israel,
Whose goings forth are from of old,
From everlasting.

Micah 5:2

Christmas would never exist without the Bible—sadly, though, at Christmastime our culture scarcely even cares.

All we know about Christ's birth is contained in the Holy Scriptures. Still, it took the arrival of these foreign pagan visitors to agitate the wicked Edomite king to finally get the religious folks excited about seeking God's revelation. How tragic that the ones who knew the prophecy so well missed the Prophesied One—only a short distance away. When they discovered the foretold location, Herod directed these noblemen to Bethlehem. What they did next shows the genuineness of their desire to worship Him.

Joy to the "Wise Men"

When they heard the king, they departed; and behold, the star which they had seen in the East went before them, till it came and stood over where the young Child was. When they saw the star, they rejoiced with exceedingly great joy.

Matthew 2:9–10

Joy and Christmas are synonymous. In the carols, joy rings aloud. In the merriment of the holidays, Christmas cheer and joy abound. Around the world we "deck the halls with boughs of holly." Sadly, much of this joy is superficial. Many who have "Merry Christmas" on their lips have hearts devoid of any joy and merriment. Not so in the case of the wise men. Matthew 2:10 tells us that when the wise men saw the star (not the store), they "rejoiced with exceedingly great joy." After their long, laborious search, the Savior's star reappears and their souls are overwhelmed by joy. Not a joy contrived of materialistic fervor; this was a soul-satisfying joy.

So great is their joy that the language of scripture amplifies it four times. Read Matthew 2:10 again: They "rejoiced with exceedingly great joy." John Piper describes this as "quadruple joy." He continues, "True worship is not just ascribing authority and dignity to Christ; it is doing this joyfully. It is doing it because you have come to see something about Christ that is so desirable that being near Him to ascribe authority and dignity to Him personally is overwhelmingly compelling."[2]

Before Jesus's birth, Elizabeth's baby leapt for joy in her womb at the voice of Mary, Jesus's mother (Luke 1:44). The angel announced the "good tidings of great joy" (Luke 2:10). We sing, "Joy to the world, the Lord is come." The fruit of the spirit is *joy* (Galatians 5:22). "In [His] presence is fullness of joy" (Psalm 16:11). The prophet Nehemiah tells us, "The joy of the LORD is your strength" (Nehemiah 8:10).

Surely this deep "joy of soul" strengthened these foreign wise men on their long journey to Jesus. Joy rang from Jesus's cradle because of the joy produced by Jesus's cross that purchased salvation and fills all believers with *joy*. "Though you have not seen him, you love him; and even though you do not see him now, you believe in him and are filled with an inexpressible and glorious joy, for you are receiving the end result of your faith, the salvation of your souls" (1 Peter 1:8–9 NIV).

The cradle promised "great joy for all people." The cross delivered on that promise. Joy motivated the Son of God to complete His ultimate mission: "Looking unto Jesus the author and finisher of our faith, who for the *joy* that was set before Him endured the cross, despising the shame, and has set down at the right hand of the throne of God" (Hebrews 12:2).

Joy surrounds the resurrected Savior, who is crowned victorious. We have joy at the cradle because of the cross. Exuberant, eternal joy abounds from the throne where He's crowned. Next time you see the word "joy" stenciled on a Christmas card or holiday decoration, take a moment and ask yourself, "Is this the joy of Jesus?" Because the true joy of Christmas *is* the joy of Jesus. It's no wonder we sing so much about joy at Christmas—like in these carols of *joy*:

Joy to the World	*Joy to the world, the Lord is come. . . . Repeat the sounding joy.*
Come, Thou Long-Expected Jesus	*Dear desire of every nation, joy of every longing heart.*
Angels We Have Heard on High	*Shepherds, why this jubilee? Why your joyous strains prolong?*
While Shepherds Watched Their Flocks by Night	*Glad tidings of great joy I bring to you and all mankind.*

Infant Holy, Infant Lowly	*Thus rejoicing, free from sorrow, praises voicing, greet the morrow.*
O Holy Night	*Sweet hymns of joy in grateful chorus raise we.*
Hark! The Herald Angels Sing	*Joyful all ye nations rise, join the triumph of the skies.*
Our Day of Joy Is Here Again	*Our day of joy is here again, with love and peace and song; come let us join th' angelic strain with voices clear and strong.*
How Great Our Joy	*This Gift of God we'll cherish well that ever joy our hearts shall fill.*
Good Christian Men Rejoice	*Good Christian men rejoice, with heart and soul and voice.*
O Come, O Come Immanuel	*Rejoice, rejoice, Immanuel shall come to you O Israel.*
God Rest Ye Merry Gentleman	*O tidings of comfort and joy, comfort and joy, O tidings of comfort and joy.*
As with Gladness Men of Old	*As with gladness men of old did the guiding star behold, as with joy they hailed its light, leading onward, beaming bright; so, most gracious Lord, may we evermore your splendor see.*

Come Adore on Bended Knee

Imagine the Magis' joy when they arrived at the birthplace of young Jesus. Matthew 2:11 states that when they saw the Son, they "fell down and worshiped Him." Cultures throughout history have bowing as part of their heritage. In fact bowing—or not bowing—in some cultures could be a matter of life or death. An act of obeisance takes many outward forms of physical lowering. It can be on a knee, on the ground, or even bending forward slightly to recognize someone. Internationally, bowing represents the giving of honor and respect. In some Asian cultures, it's common to swap cards first, and then bow to one another to the degree of rank as specified on the cards.[3] It's in the East, the origin of the wise men, that bowing is still commonly practiced to this day. These notable men would have been accustomed to people traveling from afar to bow to them. How remarkable that we find them traveling so far to fall down before Jesus!

Have you ever noticed how many Christmas carols reference a *bended* knee? We find it in lyrics like "Come, adore on bended knee, Christ the Lord, the newborn king" ("Angels We Have Heard on High") and "Fall on your knees, Oh hear the angel voices" ("O Holy Night"). Here are some others who came to Jesus on bended knee:

- Wise men—Matthew 2:11
- The leper—Mark 1:40
- The woman with a blood affliction—Mark 5:33
- The mother of the demon-possessed girl—Mark 7:25
- The demon-possessed man—Luke 8:28
- The blind man—John 9:38

One not in the above list bent the knee to Jesus, but with a quite different and tragic result. He's widely known as the rich young ruler. "Now as He was going out on the road, one came running, knelt before Him, and asked Him, 'Good Teacher, what shall I do that I may inherit eternal life?'" (Mark 10:17). But Mark 10:22 tells us how he left. "But he was sad at this word, and went away sorrowful, for he had great possessions."

Like the wise men, this young man was wealthy. We see clearly from this account that his posture of bowing was only external, not in complete submission of heart. He proudly treasured his worldly treasures over Christ, whereas the magi humbly gave their treasures to Christ.

Just as the magi bowed to Jesus and offered their valuable treasures, so we ought to be on our knees before Him with surrendered hearts. What stark contrast we see here between the hearts of the wise men and the rampant idolatry of all the material entrapments of the season. The world preaches "get and take." The Gospel gives grace to the least deserving. It changes the heart into a vessel of giving.

As with joyful steps they sped
to that lowly manger bed,
there to bend the knee before
Him, whom heaven and earth adore;
so may we with willing feet
ever seek your mercy seat.[4]

At His death, the mob also bent their knee in mockery to Him. "When they had twisted a crown of thorns, they put it on His head, and a reed in His right hand. And they bowed the knee before Him and mocked Him, saying, Hail, King of the Jews!" (Matthew 27:29). After Jesus's resurrection His followers fell down and worshiped Him. "And as they went to tell His disciples, behold, Jesus met them, saying, 'Rejoice!' So they came and held Him by the feet and worshiped Him." (Matthew 28:9).

> *Led by the light of faith serenely beaming,*
> *With glowing hearts by His cradle we stand.*
> *So led by light of a star sweetly gleaming,*
> *Here came the wise men from Orient land . . .*
> *Behold your King; before Him lowly bend!*[5]

One day "every knee shall bow" to Him (Romans 14:11). Whether it's at the cradle or the cross, everyone will "before Him prostrate fall," and "crown Him Lord of all." Regardless of culture, creed, or custom, all nations of all time will bow before the Lord. The wise men wisely bowed their bodies *and* hearts. They demonstrated their motives for seeking Jesus in the giving of gifts. Their posture reflected hearts that were changed by the little one at whose feet they bowed. The mission of Jesus would be underscored by their wise gifts.

Wise Shoppers Indeed!

The wise men had a tall task: shopping for the King of kings! What could they get Him? Matthew's Gospel tells us that when the wise men saw the star they "rejoiced with exceedingly great joy"(3:10). Verse 11 states that when they saw the Son, they "fell down and worshiped Him. And when they had opened their treasures, they presented gifts to Him: gold, frankincense, and myrrh." Their gifts reveal *why* these wise men were the wisest shoppers indeed. These gifts profoundly connect the birth of Christ to His mission.

The Gift of Gold

Gold was given to honor Christ as King. Gold is the currency of kings. When it comes to gifts for reigning kings, or infant kings, silver bells just don't stack up. It's got to be gold! King Solomon, the son of David, spared no golden expense in furnishing his own palace and especially the temple (1 Kings 10:14–21). The earthly house of God was also a house of gold.

The wise men spared no expense in their shopping for King Jesus, also the son of David, bringing Him the gift of gold.

Gold is pure, royal, and of an enduring nobility; what better item than gold to bring "glory to the newborn King"? Foreign noblemen, whom others bowed to, came a long way, but *not* to worship King Herod or Caesar Augustus—they came to honor King Jesus early in His humble life. Years later

Pilate would have "King of the Jews" inscribed on a rough-hewn shingle above His thorn-crowned head. But this Eternal King would conquer the grave to reign forever and ever.

> *Born a king on Bethlehem's plain,*
> *Gold I bring to crown Him again,*
> *King forever, ceasing never*
> *Over us all to reign.*[6]

The Gift of Frankincense

Frankincense was given to exalt His deity as the Son of God. "'Behold, the virgin shall be with child, and bear a Son, and they shall call His name Immanuel,' which is translated, 'God with us'" (Matthew 1:23). Jesus alone is worthy of worship. Worthy is the Lamb! (Revelation 5:12).

The modifying word "frank" indicates the purest incense, of highest quality. In ancient times frankincense was burned as an offering to deities. The Jews burned incense in the worship of Jehovah. In the tabernacle, and later in the temple, the priests offered incense to God. How appropriate then that Jesus is described as the Great High Priest in His perfect offering to God. Hebrews 9:11–12 states:

> *But Christ came as High Priest of the good things to*
> *come, with the greater and more perfect tabernacle not*
> *made with hands, that is, not of this creation. Not with*

the blood of goats and calves, but with His own blood
He entered the Most Holy Place once for all, having
obtained eternal redemption.

At the cross, Jesus not only performed as the perfect priest but also died as an offering for sins. The apostle Paul would later write: "And walk in love, as Christ also has loved us and given Himself for us, an offering and a sacrifice to God for a sweet-smelling aroma" (Ephesians 5:2). The wise men honored the deity of Christ, the priesthood of Christ, and the offering of Christ in this wise gift of frankincense.

Frankincense to offer have I;
incense owns a Deity nigh;
prayer and praising, voices raising,
worshipping God on high.[7]

The Gift of Myrrh

The magi offered myrrh at the cradle to honor Christ—the Son of Man. At the cross, myrrh mixed with wine was offered to the dying Savior: "Then they gave Him wine mingled with myrrh to drink, but He did not take it" (Mark 15:23). Jesus rejected the anesthesia to bear the full brunt of our sin and God's fiery wrath. He cried, "I thirst" in His last words as He finished His perfect work. The God-man would have His ravaged body anointed with myrrh and sealed in a tomb (John 19:39).

Imagine the notion of bringing a burial urn to a young child for his birthday. How would the parents and other children react to this sort of gift? This is exactly like what the wise men offered Jesus. You see, in those days and even today, burial arrangements were not cheap. Any relief would have been deeply appreciated. The God-child, however, would only need three days' worth.

At His birth, Jesus was wrapped in "swaddling clothes" and laid in a borrowed manger. At His death, the Lord was wrapped in "burial cloths" and laid in a borrowed tomb. Just as valuable myrrh came to Him at the beginning of life, so it would adorn Him at His death.

> *Myrrh is mine: its bitter perfume*
> *breathes a life of gathering gloom—*
> *sorrowing, sighing, bleeding, dying,*
> *sealed in a stone-cold tomb.*[8]

The King of Glory

Dr. John Hopkins Jr., the author of "We Three Kings of Orient Are," had no children of his own. Yet he wrote this famous carol in 1857 for a Christmas pageant that even young ones could enjoy. This hymn, his crowning work, beautifully narrates the wise men's role in the Christmas narrative. Thankfully, Hopkins did not leave Him entombed with myrrh in the grave.[9] Here's the final climactic stanza:

Glorious now behold Him arise,
King and God and sacrifice.
Alleluiah, alleluiah!
Sounds through the earth and skies.

These noble sages brought Him gifts that connected the cradle to the cross, and ultimately to the crown. Their gifts tell us the meaning of Christmas and the reason for His birth.

Treasure at the Cradle, Treasure at the Cross

At the cradle, the gift of gold
Of purest value, a currency for kings
With hearts bowed low His royalty behold
At the cross—the crown of thorns salvation brings.

Present Him frankincense, a gift for deity
Pure, sweet aroma, an offering of laud
Yet the greatest offering would be on Calvary
Where the spotless lamb bore the wrath of God.

A fragrant scent to bless the lad
A savory gift poured at His feet
At death, His body would be later clad
With swaddling clothes and myrrh so sweet.

Treasure at the cradle
Treasure at the cross

Gold, frankincense and myrrh—all for Him
The blood of the lamb shed for the lost
To give eternal life—forgiveness for sin.[10]

Gifts That Keep on Giving

How often at Christmas do we give gifts based on what others have given us in the past? We're really good at "keeping score" and oh, how we love to reciprocate! Not so with the wise men. Their gifts were thoughtful, sacrificial, unconditional, and, most importantly, Christ-centered. Remarkably each gift highlighted the mission of Jesus. Some experts even attribute modern-day Christmas gift-giving to these sagacious givers.

Another carol simplifies shopping for Jesus this way:

What can I give Him poor as I am
If I were a shepherd,
I would bring Him a Lamb
If I were a wise man,
I'd sure do my part
So what can I give Him
Give my heart.[11]

Have you opened your heart to the amazing grace offered freely by Jesus Christ? It can't be shopped for; it can't be earned. In Ephesians 2:8–9, His gift is described this way: "For by grace you have been saved through faith, and that not of yourselves; it is the gift of God, not of works, lest anyone should boast."

The wise men got it! And now we see why they were the wisest Christmas shoppers.

> *So bring Him incense, gold and myrrh,*
> *Come, peasant, king, to own Him;*
> *The King of kings salvation brings,*
> *Let loving hearts enthrone Him.*[12]

SCRIPTURE REFLECTIONS
ON THE FIRST WORDS OF JESUS

"You shall make an altar to burn incense on; you shall make it of acacia wood."

Exodus 30:1

"And when Aaron lights the lamps at twilight, he shall burn incense on it, a perpetual incense before the LORD throughout your generations."

Exodus 30:8

"I see Him, but not now;
I behold Him, but not near;
A Star shall come out of Jacob;
A Scepter shall rise out of Israel."

Numbers 24:17

The kings of Tarshish and of the isles
Will bring presents;
The kings of Sheba and Seba
Will offer gifts.
Yes, all kings shall fall down before Him;
All nations shall serve Him.

Psalm 72:10–11

Oh come, let us worship and bow down;
*Let us kneel before the L*ORD *our Maker.*

Psalm 95:6

I rejoice at Your word
As one who finds great treasure.

Psalm 119:162

The people who walked in darkness
Have seen a great light;
Those who dwelt in the land of the shadow of death,
Upon them a light has shined.

Isaiah 9:2

Arise, shine;
For your light has come!
*And the glory of the L*ORD *is risen upon you.*
For behold, the darkness shall cover the earth,
And deep darkness the people;
*But the L*ORD *will arise over you,*
And His glory will be seen upon you.
The Gentiles shall come to your light,
And kings to the brightness of your rising.

Isaiah 60:1–3

I will greatly rejoice in the LORD,
My soul shall be joyful in my God;
For He has clothed me with the garments of salvation,
He has covered me with the robe of righteousness,
As a bridegroom decks himself with ornaments,
And as a bride adorns herself with her jewels.

Isaiah 61:10

"For what will it profit a man if he gains the whole world, and loses his own soul? Or what will a man give in exchange for his soul?"

Mark 8:36–37

"Through the tender mercy of our God, with which the Dayspring from on high has visited us; to give light to those who sit in darkness and the shadow of death, to guide our feet into the way of peace."

Luke 1:78–79

And He looked up and saw the rich putting their gifts into the treasury, and He saw also a certain poor widow putting in two mites. So He said, "Truly I say to you that this poor widow has put in more than all."

Luke 21:1–3

Then Mary took a pound of very costly oil of spikenard, anointed the feet of Jesus, and wiped His feet with her hair. And the house was filled with the fragrance of the oil.

John 12:3

For you know the grace of our Lord Jesus Christ, that though He was rich, yet for your sakes He became poor, that you through His poverty might become rich.

2 Corinthians 8:9

So let each one give as he purposes in his heart, not grudgingly or of necessity; for God loves a cheerful giver.

2 Corinthians 9:7

Thanks be to God for His indescribable gift!

2 Corinthians 9:15

And so we have the prophetic word confirmed, which you do well to heed as a light that shines in a dark place, until the day dawns and the morning star rises in your hearts.

2 Peter 1:19

GROUP DISCUSSION QUESTIONS

1. What gift would you give Jesus for Christmas?

2. How were the wise men so different from the shepherds?

3. How would you describe true joy?

4. What was the significance of the magi bowing before Jesus?

5. Why the gift of gold?

6. Why the gift of frankincense?

7. Why the gift of myrrh?

Jesus is our childhood's pattern,
Day by day, like us He grew;
He was little, weak, and helpless,
Tears and smiles like us He knew:
And He feeleth our sadness,
And He shareth in our gladness.

Cecil F. Alexander
"Once in Royal David's City"

The only reason we have Christmas
is because we needed Easter.

Richard Hardee

Break forth, O beauteous heavenly light,
To herald our salvation;
He stoops to earth—the God of might,
Our hope and expectation.
He comes in human flesh to dwell,
our God with us, Immanuel,
The night of darkness ending,
Our fallen race befriending.

A. T. Russell
"Break Forth, O Beauteous Heavenly Light"

O sing a song of Calvary, its glory and dismay;
Of Him who hung upon the tree,
And took our sins away.
For He who died on Calvary is risen from the grave,
And Christ, our Lord, by heav'n adored, is mighty now to save.

Louis F. Benson
"O Sing a Song of Bethlehem"

CHAPTER SIX

PURPOSE-DRIVEN JESUS

S hould we cancel church services on Christmas Sunday?
Are you kidding me?!

This topic lit up my talk show one year when Christmas Day happened to fall on a Sunday. What a show it was! The lighthearted conversation quickly escalated into an intense discussion. Some folks were even mad at their preacher for *not* canceling services. After all, they argued, "Isn't Christmas about waking up with your family, enjoying a big breakfast and opening presents, followed by a trip to Grandma's house?" How dare we interrupt such sacred Christmas traditions with church? Not to mention the fact that Christmas Day on the weekend doesn't give me that extra day off work! It's one thing to attend the church Christmas program a few weeks out, or even drop by the Christmas Eve service, but a Christmas service on the Lord's Day? Well, that may be taking things too far!

Isn't this exactly the issue, and not just on Christmas Day

but every day? If Jesus really is who He claims to be, then He's not just the reason for the season, but the reason for life! He's the reason we even have church. In fact, He *invented* church! These kinds of conversations certainly remind us of how far we have fallen from centering Christmas on Christ and His purpose, instead of on our own personal "celebrations."

Of course, we say the baby Jesus is the central figure of Christmas. But how often do we smother Him under everything else that crowds our life? In His first words, He tells us why He came and why He is the central figure at Christmas and *all the time*. Though Christmas may be the only time the world speaks of Him, the scope of His mission is so much bigger and grander, and it brought Him in touch with men and women who helped shape His world—and ours.

The Mission of Jesus

"Will he be an astronaut, a famous politician, an athlete, inventor, or a doctor?" No sooner than the congratulations and celebrations commence at the birth of a child, the speculations about the future begin. We know that DNA, upbringing, culture, and many other factors influence a child's ultimate calling. Most importantly, parents want to know, "What will he accomplish in life?" In the case of the God-baby, His God-sized purpose was set before birth. He was prophesied to be the Redeemer-seed of the woman in Genesis 3:15. The prophet Isaiah spoke of His virgin birth centuries before in Isaiah 7:14. From all eternity, Jesus Christ remained faithful to His purpose. Once on earth, He was never distracted, diverted, or sidetracked. He was on mission to be the Savior of the world. He followed His Father's calling from the cradle to the cross, and He lived perfectly on mission to ultimately wear the crown.

His mission was His Father's will:

- "Did you not know that I must be about My Father's business?" (Luke 2:49).
- "My Father has been working until now, and I have been working" (John 5:17).
- "The Father has not left Me alone, for I always do those things that please Him" (John 8:29).
- "My Father, if this cup cannot pass away from Me unless I drink it, Your will be done" (Matthew 26:42).
- "I have finished the work which You have given Me to do" (John 17:4).

First Words of Joseph

When a child is born, the father is often looked to for words of welcome and wisdom. While Joseph was not Jesus's father, he would be his earthly guide and mentor—the male role model in Jesus's earthly life. Joseph is mentioned very little in Scripture, and mainly in the Christmas passages. He's only referenced in a handful of carols and hymns. But what were his first words? Matthew 1:25 records he "did not know her till she had brought forth her firstborn Son. And he called

121

His name Jesus." So the only specific words, or actually word, Joseph is credited with saying is a name, the name of Jesus. He might have been a man of few words, but his life was clearly centered on the one whose "Name is above all names."

Every time we meet this man, he is on God's mission—usually as revealed in a dream. He could have easily "cut and run" from Mary at the news of her pregnancy. Where I grew up, it's still fairly common for the young man to "do the right thing" and marry his pregnant girlfriend. Not so in those times. Jewish law considered the "right thing" to be something as severe as execution by stoning. After all, this wasn't even Joseph's baby to start with!

Yet Joseph believed God and followed Him faithfully. This humble carpenter raised Jesus as his own son, and also trusted Jesus as Savior. Like Mary, Joseph would serve a dual role in bringing up the One who would "save His people—including Joseph and Mary—from their sins." The Savior of the world grew up in a carpenter's home whose only recorded word was "Jesus."

The Perfect Child

Only one baby has ever been perfect. Only one child has ever been the perfect child. Before He was the God-man, Jesus Christ was the God-embryo. He would become the God-baby and then the God-toddler, and the God-teenager. Every step of the way, Jesus was perfect, without sin, and only performed righteous deeds. Imagine being his younger half-sibling. He never started a fight with one of them. When conflict broke out, it was never *His* fault. How many times would Mary and Joseph have to scold the other children with the words, "Why can't you be like your older brother?" He never made trouble at play or temple. Yes, it *was* always the other kids. He was no angel, for He made the angels, and *they* worshiped Him (Hebrews 1:6). He was the only child worthy of having the "world revolve around Him," because He, in fact, put the world into orbit. With all the selfishness and indulgence at Christmastime, the One who brings us Christmas was perfectly selfless. Never self-centered, He was always God centered—for He was the very gift of God (Romans 5:8).

The Christ-child was also the only perfect child ever adopted by an imperfect stepfather. He was the only child who deserved the worship of His parents. Faced with every temptation young men face—yet He was perfectly obedient and holy. He was "in all points tempted as we are, yet without sin" (Hebrews 4:15). From the beginning, He was *always* about His Father's business!

The world could have seen this perfect child as the next great leader—one with incredible potential to do amazing things. His mission, however, was something far more important. Luke 19:10 says, "The Son of Man has come to seek and to save that which was lost." Jesus was not perfect for the sake of being perfect. He was perfect because He was God, and only a perfect sacrifice could save the lost.

Thou camest, O Lord, with the living word
That should set thy people free,
But with mocking scorn and with crown of thorn
They bore Thee to Calvary.[1]

From the glories of heaven He descended into our impoverished world to save lost and hopeless sinners. He spoke frequently of His mission—while every force of hell and earth was trying to take Him off course. With no room in the inn, He had barely a place to be born. Then as a toddler, He and His family fled as refugees to a foreign land (Matthew 2:14–16). One of the most powerful "mission moments" came in the early life of Jesus when His parents took Him to the temple to be dedicated. There they encountered two fascinating characters.

A Baby on My Bucket List

What's on your bucket list? "Bucket list" is a phrase many use to describe the things they hope to see or accomplish before they die. Or to put it more bluntly, "Stuff you really want to do before you kick the bucket."

The answer to this question will indicate a lot about your priorities in life. It will speak volumes to your values and passions. Most of all, your bucket list may best define your mission. For the elderly man and woman, Simeon and Anna, in the Christmas story, their bucket list was laser focused! It was seeing a baby. Beholding the infant Jesus consumed and overwhelmed them. Though we know very little about these two, Simeon encountered Jesus first and his life's mission was fulfilled:

> *And, behold, there was a man in Jerusalem, whose name was Simeon; and the same man was just and devout, waiting for the consolation of Israel: and the Holy Ghost was upon him. And it was revealed unto him by the Holy Ghost, that he should not see death, before he had seen the Lord's Christ. And he came by the Spirit into the temple: and when the parents brought in the child Jesus, to do for him after the custom of the law, then took he him up in his arms, and blessed God, and said, Lord, now lettest thou thy servant depart in peace, according to thy word: For mine eyes have seen thy salvation, which thou hast prepared before the face of all people; a light to lighten the Gentiles, and the glory of thy people Israel. And Joseph and his mother marvelled at those things which were spoken of him. And Simeon blessed them, and said unto Mary his mother, Behold, this child is set for the fall and rising again of many in Israel; and for a sign which shall be spoken against; (Yea, a sword shall pierce through thy own soul also,) that the thoughts of many hearts may be revealed.*
>
> Luke 2:25–35 KJV

We're told even less about godly Anna:

> *Now there was one, Anna, a prophetess, the daughter of Phanuel, of the tribe of Asher. She was of a great age, and had lived with a husband seven years from her virginity; and this woman was a widow of about eighty-four years, who did not depart from the temple, but served God with fastings and prayers night and day. And coming in that instant she gave thanks to the Lord, and spoke of Him to all those who looked for redemption in Jerusalem.*
>
> Luke 2:36–38

Both of these godly characters were in their golden years of life. Both knew their days on earth were coming to an end. Both were consumed with seeing Jesus; "the hopes and fears" of all their years were met in Him that day. Because of the work of Jesus, both Simeon and Anna are now beholding His glory in heaven.

All the Way to the Cross
Theologians and Hollywood may speculate about Jesus's youth, but in reality, all that is known about it are the profound words of mission we encounter in Luke 2. However, we can see the incredible connection between His words and His mission in the Gospels. In His teaching, He was on

mission. In His travels, He was on mission. Even in the face of betrayal, torture, and execution, He was on mission.

> *Pilate therefore said to Him, "Are You a king then?"*
> *Jesus answered, "You say rightly that I am a king. For*
> *this cause I was born, and for this cause I have come*
> *into the world, that I should bear witness to the truth.*
> *Everyone who is of the truth hears My voice."*
>
> John 18:37

The boy from the temple at the earlier Passover feast now declared His mission to the Roman governor of Judea. But at this Passover, He was the lamb to be slain. "So when Jesus had received the sour wine, He said, 'It is finished'" (John 19:30).

What did He finish? In His last moments on the cross, He triumphantly declared victorious completion of His mission. In His dying words, Jesus Christ made the greatest closing statement of all time. What appears as three words in English is actually only one word in Greek, *Tetelesti*, a word of eternal exclamation, closure, and victory. He fulfilled all righteousness (Matthew 3:15). Every prophecy is hence fulfilled, every command is kept, and every good deed done. The cradle is finished and now the cross is finished!

With this word, He lays aside the crown of thorns and is crowned "Lord of all." Hail the heaven-born Prince of

Peace, and "glory to the newborn King." Come, let us adore the *only* One who perfectly accomplished that which no one else could: "God and sinners reconciled." He was about His Father's business perfectly in birth, perfectly in life, in death and in resurrection splendor. He finished His mission to reconcile lost sinners into the saving knowledge of the Father.

The Only Performance That Counts

Christmastime is jam-packed with performances. While you're off enjoying a summer vacation at the beach, your music pastor is working hard on the church's annual Christmas program. No sooner than that Thanksgiving feast is digested, the Epperson family, like most families, gets in full gear for one Christmas show after another. Handel's *Messiah, The Festival of Lights,* our church's event, the kids' multiple school plays. So many performances dominate the season. Isn't this like life? From the moment you're born till the moment you pass into eternity, you are performing. Life is like a play in which everyone is an actor.

As a kid, you're asked, "What do you want to do when you grow up?" All through school students are deluged with questions about their career, calling, and plans for the future. And, yes, there's a reason they're called "tests" and "grades." Whether you're "knee-high" in kindergarten or ninety years old on the golf course, everyone's keeping score. Maybe you're a "ChrEaster"—a Christmas- and Easter-only Christian. You hope you can score points with the big man upstairs by popping into His house a couple of times a year.

Sadly, in God's economy, no such category exists. The problem is, no one shoots an eighteen in golf. No one remembers every line. No human has ever performed or achieved perfectly. In fact, every motivational speaker I've ever heard bases success on the many failures along the way.

The Bible says, "There is none righteous, no, not one" and "all have sinned and fall short of the glory of God" (Romans 3:10, 23). Even the Christian life, a life supposedly based on God's amazing grace, becomes a performance maze for many believers. We're far more prone to act as "human doings" than human beings. "Behaving" can quickly replace "believing." We much prefer to focus on what we "do for Him" rather than what "He has done for us." Believers tend to run to and fro to earn the approval of God and others. "Yes, I'm saved by grace, but now it's time to get to work so God will love me more." This mind-set goes against everything that the Christ of Christmas came for.

This is also why the apostle Paul strongly chastised the church at Galatia when he wrote, "O foolish Galatians! Who has bewitched you that you should not obey the truth. . . . Are you so foolish? Having begun in the Spirit, are you now being made perfect by the flesh?" (Galatians 3:1–3).

So why the performance treadmill? Fundamentally, we lose sight of the complete performance of the only One who performed completely. The Gospel is not only good news because it gets one "in the door" of the faith. It's so much bigger. It's the power of God to grant new birth and sustain new life—all emanating from the perfect life of Jesus. He makes the sinner a son and then sustains him on the *Pilgrim's Progress* all the way to glory! And it's all based on Him. What He has done.

His achievement is the *one* and only *one* performance that ultimately matters for all eternity. Because only the performance of Jesus was absolutely perfect.

In his book *Transforming Grace*, Jerry Bridges observes, "We give lip service to the attitude of the apostle Paul, 'But by the grace of God I am what I am' (1 Corinthians 15:10), but our unspoken motto is, 'God helps those who help themselves.' The realization that my daily relationship with God is based on the infinite merit of Christ is a very freeing and joyous experience. But it is not meant to be a one-time experience; the truth needs to be reaffirmed daily."[2]

Another reason we miss this truth is that we isolate His work on the cross as His only performance that counts. Jesus was about His Father's business from all eternity and in His first breath of nativity. Although the cross and the resurrection triumphantly demonstrate the climactic finale of His performance, the scriptures tell us there's more. Jesus's suffering and work for lost sinners was not only at Calvary but also at Bethlehem and everywhere in between. Before He suffered the humility of death by crucifixion, He entered our fallen world in the humility of birth in a stable. The book of Hebrews tells us, "Therefore, in all things He had to be made like His brethren, that He might be a merciful and faithful High Priest in things pertaining to God, to make propitiation for the sins of the people. For in that He Himself has suffered, being tempted, He is able to aid those who are tempted" (Hebrews 2:17–18).

And Hebrews 4:15 reminds us that He was "in all points tempted as we are, yet without sin." The author of Hebrews goes on with this same thought in chapter 5: "Though He was a Son, yet He learned obedience by the things which He suffered. And having been perfected, He became the author of eternal salvation to all who obey Him" (Hebrews 5:8–9).

Romans also teaches that we are saved by His entire life: "For if when we were enemies we were reconciled to God through the death of His Son, much more, having been reconciled, we shall be saved by His life" (Romans 5:10).

Everything Jesus thought, said, and performed as a child, as a young boy, and as a grown man was done in perfect righteousness. Including everything He didn't do. He was the spotless Lamb without blemish. His perfect work was not limited just to the cradle or the cross, but encompassed all of His very life.

In his letter to the Philippians, Paul takes us through the entire process, from Jesus's humiliation to His coronation:

> *But [He] made Himself of no reputation, taking the form of a bondservant, and coming in the likeness of*

men. And being found in appearance as a man, He humbled Himself and became obedient to the point of death, even the death of the cross. Therefore God also has highly exalted Him and given Him the name which is above every name, that at the name of Jesus every knee should bow, of those in heaven, and of those on earth, and of those under the earth, and that every tongue should confess that Jesus Christ is Lord, to the glory of God the Father.

Philippians 2:7–11

Hence, those who trust in Him for salvation get the whole performance of Jesus applied to their life. In Galatians 2:20 Paul tells us that living "crucified with Christ" means that the "life which I now live in the flesh I live by faith in the Son of God, who loved me and gave Himself for me."

Theologian R. C. Sproul articulates this profound doctrine in this way:

Jesus not only had to die for our sins, but He had to live for our righteousness. His life of perfect obedience is just as necessary for our salvation as His perfect atonement on the cross. Because there's double imputation. My sin to Him, His righteousness to me. So that is what the scripture is getting at when it says Jesus is our righteousness.[3]

Are you living as one clothed in His perfect righteousness? It means knowing Him and "abiding" daily in Him (John 15:5). The abundant fruit of His accomplishments from the virgin's womb to the empty tomb will shine through you into others—and they'll know you've been with Jesus (Acts 4:13).

Knowing Him is central to this, as we learn from a passionate Paul in Philippians 3.

Five Powerful Words

The apostle Paul knew all about God, and he had earned the top religious credentials available (Philippians 3:2–4). Despite these things, he counted all of his pedigrees as "worthless" compared to the "Excellency of the knowledge of Christ Jesus my Lord" (Philippians 3:7–8 KJV). What a powerful statement!

The passage climaxes with Paul's purpose in life: "That I may know Him and the power of His resurrection, and the fellowship of His sufferings, being conformed to His death, if, by any means, that I may attain to the resurrection of the dead" (v. 10).

Take a moment to ponder these first five powerful words of Philippians 3:10: "That I may know Him." Anyone who takes these words seriously and makes them a life mission will be changed forever! There is no situation, problem, or issue that knowing Jesus can't solve. He is all and everything. Knowing Him brings us into union with Him as verse 9 says:

"And be found in Him." So essential is this to the life of the Christian, the phrase "in Him" or "in Christ" occurs more than 160 times in the New Testament. This is why He came to us in a manger at Christmas . . . *that I may know him.*

Four Powerful Purposes

In the next words of Philippians 3:10, Paul amplifies this supernatural relationship with Christ in four ways. The first is "the power of His resurrection." Just as the Holy Spirit miraculously conceived the baby Jesus in Mary's womb, so Jesus is born in us by an act of the divine. Romans 8:14 says that those who are quickened by the "Spirit of God, these are sons of God." The resurrection power that raised Jesus from the dead raises dead sinners to life and salvation (Ephesians 2:1). The same power also supernaturally fuels the Christian's life of faith.

Second, knowing Him involves the fellowship of His suffering. Christ suffered from the rough setting at His birthday to a life of pain, temptation, rejection, and ultimately death by crucifixion. When you know Him, you know the "Man of sorrows and acquainted with grief" (Isaiah 53:3). Knowing Him is taking on His cross. The Greek word translated "fellowship" comes from the same word from which we derive our English word "partnership." This intimates a special union believers have with Jesus, as He meets us in our deepest pain. As C. S. Lewis once said, "God whispers to us in our pleasures, speaks in our conscience, but shouts in our pain."[4]

Paul describes the third aspect of knowing him as knowing "the likeness of His death" (Romans 6:5). It was Paul who earlier in Philippians 1:21 said, "For to me, to live is Christ, and to die is gain." When Jesus invites us to follow Him, it involves taking up our cross—an instrument of death. The Christian is someone whom Galatians 2:20 says has been "crucified with Christ." Knowing Jesus radically changes how we view death. It's been said that for the unbeliever this life on earth is the best it will ever be, but for the believer it's the worst it will ever be, because of the amazing hope of heaven. Death for the Christian is transition into perfection and life eternal—fully knowing Jesus, without the frailty of our flesh (1 Corinthians 13:12). The Christ child came into the humanity of our flesh to ultimately deliver us from that frailty. We may eagerly warm up to the crib of Christ, but the cross of Christ is just as critical to knowing Him.

Finally, Paul connects knowing Jesus to attaining the resurrection of the dead. Just as His resurrection power saves the sinners in the new birth, so all those saints will be raised forever to reign with Jesus. "When Christ who is our life appears, then you also will appear with Him in glory" (Colossians 3:4). Few followers of God have suffered like the ancient Bible character Job. Yet even in the fire of his pain and trials, Job held strong to the hope of resurrection, "For I know that my Redeemer lives, and He shall stand at last on the earth" (Job 19:25). Jesus conquered death to make us "more than conquerors" (Romans 8:37).

One of our family's favorite Christmas traditions is attending Handel's *Messiah* at Christmastime. My favorite part is when the bass vocalist sings out, "The trumpet shall sound, and the dead shall be raised, be raised incorruptible." Most remarkably, the entire mood of the auditorium changes at the sound of these triumphal words. The Lord is risen indeed! Praise be to God that those who know Him, will be raised *with* Him (1 Corinthians 15:51–52).

> *Behold, I tell you a mystery: We shall not all sleep, but we shall all be changed—in a moment, in the twinkling of an eye, at the last trumpet. For the trumpet will sound, and the dead will be raised incorruptible, and we shall be changed.*
>
> 1 Corinthians 15:51–52

Receive the Total Package

Many know about Him. Just about everyone has some knowledge of the Christmas baby. Only those who know Him personally are transformed now and forever. I once heard a preacher say, "Don't miss heaven by eighteen inches!" That's the distance from your head to your heart. The knowledgeable and spiritually gifted ones of Matthew 7 were thrown into hell with this simple description: "I never knew you; depart from Me" (Matthew 7:23).

Knowing Him is experiencing new life in Christ and taking on His life. Your passion becomes all about who He is and all that He accomplishes in His mission. The Gospel brings undeserving sinners into relationship with God, based solely on what He has done for us in Christ, not what we do for Him. Only there do we find our true purpose. His purpose in coming to the cradle and going all the way to the cross was to make a way for us to know Him personally and intimately. *This* was His Father's business.

Only in Him are we complete and is our identity defined. Paul says it so well in Colossians, "For in Him dwells all the fullness of the Godhead bodily; and you are complete in Him, who is the head of all principality and power" (Colossians 2:9–10).

Have you received the total package and trusted in Him completely? He alone can save you from yourself, your sins, and God's wrath. Stop trying to earn the gift and receive His perfect gift of forgiveness.

"In Him we have redemption through His blood, the forgiveness of sins, according to the riches of His grace" (Ephesians 1:7). How many of us—as with some of the callers on my controversial talk show topic—get everything right about Christmas *except* Christ? We're more focused on our Christmas traditions than on Jesus's Christmas mission. How easily we forget that *every* day is the Lord's—including December 25th. He's not asking to be a convenient minor addition or the reason for another day off. He offers you everything, and knowing Him is the greatest consuming passion anyone can have. He is the King of kings and Lord of lords.

The joy He brings was experienced by the shepherds, the wise men, Mary and Joseph, Simeon and Anna—once they encountered Jesus for who He really was. Herod was so close to the One who could save him, but he tragically died in his own darkness. What about you? Is He your King and your Lord? Believe on Him today and let your destiny be forever bound to the One who was "born to die" so that you might be reborn and live forever. He conquered sin and death and offers you the joy of life everlasting.

> *Now ye hear of endless bliss: Joy! Joy!*
> *Jesus Christ was born for this!*
> *He has opened heaven's door,*
> *and man is blessed ever more*
> *Christ was born for this!*
> *Christ was born for this!*[5]

Are you ready to go with Him past the cradle into His very life? He is calling you *now* to follow Him. God did not send a program, a plan, or a practice to redeem lost souls. He sent a *person*. His name is Jesus. He was about His Father's business, to bring fallen, lost, and broken sinners into a personal intimacy with Himself.

> *For God so loved the world that He gave His only begotten Son, that whoever believes in Him should not*

perish but have everlasting life. For God did not send His Son into the world to condemn the world, but that the world through Him might be saved.

John 3:16–17

Do you know Him?

SCRIPTURE REFLECTIONS
ON THE FIRST WORDS OF JESUS

Then I said, "Behold, I come;
In the scroll of the book it is written of me.
I delight to do Your will, O my God,
And Your law is within my heart."

Psalm 40:7–8

Thus says the LORD:
   "Let not the wise man glory in his wisdom,
   Let not the mighty man glory in his might,
   Nor let the rich man glory in his riches;
   But let him who glories glory in this,
   That he understands and knows Me."

Jeremiah 9:23–24

But Jesus called them to Himself and said to them, "You know that those who are considered rulers over the Gentiles lord it over them, and their great ones exercise authority over them. Yet it shall not be so among you; but whoever desires to become great among you shall be your servant. And whoever of you desires to be first shall be slave of all. For even the Son of Man did not come to be served, but to serve, and to give His life a ransom for many."

Mark 10:42–45

"The Father loves the Son, and has given all things into His hand. He who believes in the Son has everlasting life; and he who does not believe the Son shall not see life, but the wrath of God abides on him."

John 3:35–36

And Jesus said to them, "I am the bread of life. He who comes to Me shall never hunger, and he who believes in Me shall never thirst. But I said to you that you have seen Me and yet do not believe. All that the Father gives Me will come to Me, and the one who comes to Me I will by no means cast out. For I have come down from heaven, not to do My own will, but the will of Him who sent Me. This is the will of the Father who sent Me, that of all He has given Me I should lose nothing, but should raise it up at the last day. And this is the will of Him who sent Me, that everyone who sees the Son and believes in Him may have everlasting life; and I will raise him up at the last day."

John 6:35–40

Jesus answered and said to them, "Even if I bear witness of Myself, My witness is true, for I know where I came from and where I am going; but you do not know where I come from and where I am going."

John 8:14

"I must work the works of Him who sent Me while it is day; the night is coming when no one can work. As long as I am in the world, I am the light of the world."

John 9:4–5

"Now My soul is troubled, and what shall I say? 'Father, save Me from this hour'? But for this purpose I came to this hour. Father, glorify Your name." Then a voice came from heaven, saying, "I have both glorified it and will glorify it again."

John 12:27–28

"And this is eternal life, that they may know You, the only true God, and Jesus Christ whom You have sent. I have glorified You on the earth. I have finished the work which You have given Me to do."

John 17:3–4

So Jesus said to Peter, "Put your sword into the sheath. Shall I not drink the cup which My Father has given Me?"

John 18:11

Though He was a Son, yet He learned obedience by the things which He suffered. And having been perfected, He became the author of eternal salvation to all who obey Him.

Hebrews 5:8–9

GROUP DISCUSSION QUESTIONS

1. What would you do about church if Christmas Day fell on the Lord's Day?

2. What's significant about Joseph's first word?

3. How do Anna and Simeon's bucket lists communicate their values and mission?

4. What was the mission of Jesus?

5. How do the first five words of Philippians 3:10 connect you to Jesus's mission?

6. What does it mean to "know" Him?

7. How can you receive the ultimate gift of salvation?

Bless all the dear children in Thy tender care,
And fit us for heaven, to live with you there.

John T. McFarland
"Away in a Manger"

Ah, dearest Jesus, holy Child,
Make Thee a bed, soft, undefiled,
Within my heart, that it may be
A quiet chamber kept for Thee.

Martin Luther
"From Heaven Above to Earth I Come"

How silently, how silently the wondrous gift is given!
So God imparts to human hearts the blessings of His heaven.
No ear may hear His coming, but in this world of sin,
Where meek souls will receive Him still,
our dear Christ enters in.

Phillips Brooks
"O Little Town of Bethlehem"

Into my manger His life is born
My broken heart—His Bethlehem.
Come fill my darkness oh morning light
Be born in me this holy night.

Stu Epperson Jr.

CHAPTER SEVEN

'TWAS THE DAY AFTER CHRISTMAS

To the consumer Christmas Day is the end. To the believer Christmas Day is only the beginning.

'Twas the day after Christmas
And all through the world
The shepherds were spreading
His glorious word.

Good news of the savior
In the fullness of time
Born in a manger
To redeem mankind.

The prince of heaven
Would go to the cross

To purchase salvation
And ransom the lost.

Alive from the grave
The king would emerge
In victorious power
He'll one day return. [1]

Angels and Shepherds

Without angels and shepherds, it would be difficult, if not impossible, to cast a Christmas performance. They dominate the sacred hymns and carols. Angels announced His birth, and shepherds were the first responders and missionaries. Only Almighty God could construct a narrative where these grand occupants of heaven interact with these humblest of earth dwellers. We only know one of the Christmas angels' names—Gabriel. We'll never know, until we reach heaven, the names of the shepherds. The prominence they share in the Christmas narrative richly instructs us on the true meaning of Christmas and the ultimate meaning of life. They both were all about His Father's business.

Angels Among Us

My little angels were spectacular! Possibly the best Christmas ever was the year when all four of our daughters—Hope, Gracie, Joy, and Faith—were in the church's Christmas pageant. Of course, *all* my girls are angels, but only the two oldest actually played the role of angels. Such a role finds its entire significance in magnifying the star of the story. They were the ultimate supporting cast, shining their light (and wings) on the baby Jesus. They had one purpose, to draw maximum attention to the Savior, and to highlight His mission.

The same is true of the angels in the Christmas story and throughout the Bible. They are never the focus, but are always focused on, and centered on, their King! Yes, Christmas is great, because the Savior is great. To make much of Him, the heavenly hosts were summoned, and what great glory they shone all around! Their light pointed to the brilliance of the light of Christ. On Christmas Eve, as long as I can remember, our family has attended the Moravian Love Feast at the Home Moravian Church in Historic Old Salem. This centuries-old tradition is full of hymns about the angels, the shepherds, Mary and Joseph, and all the elements surrounding His advent. The service climaxes with the lighting of the candles. As everyone, young and old, holds up candles, the Light of the world is exalted. Every year, we all agree that "Morning Star," led by the children's choir, is our favorite song. Because it magnifies Christ so beautifully, I'm sure the angels would enjoy singing along as well:

> *Morning Star, Thy glory bright*
> *far excels the sun's clear light.*
> *Jesus be, constantly,*

Constantly, Jesus be
more than thousand suns to me.[2]

All those bound for Bethlehem that night of advent, found that "in her dark street shineth the everlasting light." In the stable, the Light of the world was shining brightest from the humblest of posts.

The star of the Christmas story, though a babe, created all the other cast members. First among His creations were the angels. And they were created to serve and worship Him (Hebrews 1:6). Look at the unique role played by these heavenly hosts:

- In the beginning with God before creation (Job 38:7)
- Active throughout the Old Testament (Genesis 3:24)
- Heralded His humble birth (Luke 2:9–14)
- Ministered to Him in the wilderness (Matthew 4:11; Mark 1:13)
- Strengthened Him in the Garden of Gethsemane (Luke 22:43)
- Stood by at His gruesome death (Matthew 26:53)
- The first to proclaim His resurrection (Matthew 28:2–6; Luke 24:4–7)
- The first to speak after His ascension (Acts 1:10–11)
- Present and active in the book of Acts with the early Church (Acts 12:7–19)

- Observe the propriety of church worship services (1 Corinthians 11:10)
- Long to look into the heavenly revelations of God (1 Peter 1:12)
- Active in return of Christ and judgment (Matthew 13:41–43)

The angels saw it all. They worshiped Him since the time of their creation. They were with His prophet Daniel in the lions' den (Daniel 6:22), and overwhelmed Isaiah in a mighty vision (Isaiah 6:1–7). They announced Jesus's grand entrance into time and space. They sustained Him in His mission to save. Angels, more than any other created beings, fully supported the mission of Jesus. They remain active to this day, and their tune hasn't changed one bit. No figures are more committed to wholeheartedly serving His mission.

Sing, Choir of Angels

Can you name a sacred Christmas hymn or carol that does *not* have any mention of angels? The overwhelming majority of carols reference them. Only a handful of them don't. You may be surprised to learn that carols mention "angels" more often than Mary, Joseph, and the wise men combined. How appropriate that at Christmastime we sing the most about the ones who first sang that original Christmas Day.

These heavenly messengers are such a critical part of the

Christmas narrative. Angels headline the titles of some more popular carols like:

"Hark! The Herald Angels Sing"

"Angels We Have Heard on High"

"Angels from the Realms of Glory"

They play a key role in so many other songs of Christmas:

- *Sing choirs of angels, sing in adoration. O sing all ye bright hosts of heaven above.* —"O Come, All Ye Faithful"
- *Fall on your knees, Oh hear the angel voices.* —"O Holy Night!"
- *The first Noel the angel did say, was to certain poor sinners in fields as they lay.* —"The First Noel"
- *Let heaven and nature sing.* —"Joy to the World"
- *Glories stream from heaven afar, heavenly hosts sing alleluia.* —"Silent Night"
- *While by the sheep we watched at night, glad tidings brought an angel bright.* —"How Great Our Joy"
- *Swift are winging angels singing, noels ringing, tidings bringing.* —"Infant Holy, Infant Lowly"
- *We hear the Christmas angels, the great glad tidings tell.* —"O Little Town of Bethlehem"
- *Or all of God's angels in heaven to sing.* —"I Wonder as I Wander"
- *The shepherds feared and trembled, when lo! above the*

> *earth, rang out the angel chorus that hailed the Savior's birth.* —"Go Tell It on the Mountain"
- *Whom angels greet with anthems sweet, while shepherds watch are keeping.* —"What Child Is This?"
- *The angel of the Lord came down, and glory shone around.* — "While Shepherds Watched Their Flocks"
- *From angels bending near the earth to touch their harps of gold.* —"It Came Upon the Midnight Clear"
- *Heaven's arches rang when the angels sang proclaiming thy royal decree.* —"Thou Didst Leave Thy Throne"

Angels are in so many Christmas carols because they're so central to the biblical account of Christmas.

What Did the Angels Say?

There's no question the angels were about the Father's business. Simply listening to their words reveals this. If you removed all the Bible's nativity references of the angels—especially their message—you'd find very little left of the Christmas story. Let's hear from the angels on high. Gabriel's first words to Joseph dominate the first chapter of Matthew.

> *But while he thought about these things, behold, an angel of the Lord appeared to him in a dream, saying, "Joseph, son of David, do not be afraid to take to you Mary your wife, for that which is conceived in her is of*

the Holy Spirit. And she will bring forth a Son, and you shall call His name JESUS, for He will save His people from their sins." So all this was done that it might be fulfilled which was spoken by the Lord through the prophet, saying: "Behold, the virgin shall be with child, and bear a Son, and they shall call His name Immanuel," which is translated, "God with us."

Matthew 1:20–23

Later an angel came in another dream to warn Joseph,

Now when they had departed, behold, an angel of the Lord appeared to Joseph in a dream, saying, "Arise, take the young Child and His mother, flee to Egypt, and stay there until I bring you word; for Herod will seek the young Child to destroy Him."

Matthew 2:13

In Luke 1:28, 30–33, 35–37 the angel's words to Mary connect the Old and New Testaments. The angel speaks of profound doctrines such as the virgin birth, the incarnation, the salvation of humankind, and some of the richest Christology (doctrine of Christ) in the New Testament:

And having come in, the angel said to her, "Rejoice, highly favored one, the Lord is with you; blessed are you among women!" Then the angel said to her "Do not be afraid, Mary, for you have found favor with God. And behold, you will conceive in your womb and bring forth a Son, and shall call His name JESUS. He will be great, and will be called the Son of the Highest; and the Lord God will give Him the throne of His father David. And He will reign over the house of Jacob forever, and of His kingdom there will be no end."

And finally, the angel answered Mary's question, "How can this be?":

And the angel answered and said to her, "The Holy Spirit will come upon you, and the power of the Highest will overshadow you; therefore, also, that Holy One who is to be born will be called the Son of God. Now indeed, Elizabeth your relative has also conceived a son in her old age; and this is now the sixth month for her who was called barren. For with God nothing will be impossible."

The angel's proclamation to the shepherds is the basis for many of our Christmas songs and messages:

And behold, an angel of the Lord stood before them, and the glory of the Lord shone around them, and they were greatly afraid. Then the angel said to them, "Do not be afraid, for behold, I bring you good tidings of great

*joy which will be to all people. For there is born to you
this day in the city of David a Savior, who is Christ the
Lord. And this will be the sign to you: You will find a
Babe wrapped in swaddling cloths, lying in a manger."
And suddenly there was with the angel a multitude
of the heavenly host praising God and saying: "Glory
to God in the highest, And on earth peace, goodwill
toward men!"*

Luke 2:9–14

So much detail of the Savior's birth comes out of the
mouths of angels. They tell us:

- who Jesus is
- why Jesus came
- where He was born
- how He came
- how He fulfilled prophecy
- His return and future dominion

Angels also play an important role in Jesus's life, resurrection, and mission. Most notably, angels are the only characters in the Christmas narrative that appear before His birth, throughout His earthly ministry, after His resurrection, and at His future coronation and return. At the beginning, we see them present in the Garden of Eden (Genesis 3:24). At the end of times, we find angels lighting up the book of Revelation with more than eighty references to the word "angel."[3] In

Genesis, angels guarded the Tree of Life after man's ejection from the Garden. In Revelation, they celebrate the Tree of Life as they accompany the conquering King Jesus. Angels exist to serve the mission of Jesus. The single best definition of their purpose is found in Hebrews 1:14: "Are they not all ministering spirits sent forth to minister for those who will inherit salvation?"

Hebrews gives more definitions for the angels' roles than any book in the Bible. These were no chubby baby cherubs. Though not omnipotent or all-powerful like God, angels are powerful beings. Anytime they appear in Scripture, their presence is surely felt. Courage quickly returned to Elisha's dismayed servant when his eyes were opened to the chariots of angels protecting them from a fierce Syrian army on all sides (2 Kings 6:16–18). A single angel wiped out an entire army of 185,000 Assyrian soldiers in minutes (2 Kings 19:35).

Everywhere you see these heavenly messengers, you find them carrying out the mission of God—from creation to the cradle to the cross to the crown.

Angels at the Cross

Imagine having to stand by and watch the one you were sent to serve be ruthlessly executed. This was exactly the case on that first Good Friday. There, at the cross of Christ, we find the angels strangely silent and inactive. They stood down at the height of the Savior's greatest suffering. Why this restraint? Why not engage, at the ultimate battle scene of all time, when all the forces of evil attacked the object of their worship? In finishing His divine mission, the Lord Jesus was not only forsaken by His heavenly Father (Mark 15:34), He was also without the aid of His heavenly servants.

No relief came from the heavenly warriors. They must have been confounded at the sight of their bloodied, dying Master. Perhaps they reasoned, *Why can't we help? Just one of us could wipe out the whole lot of these evil beasts!* Or, *What's so special about these humans that our Lord helplessly suffers in their place?* First Peter 1:10–12 provides some insight. Peter recounts the redemption story, from the prophets all the way to Jesus fulfilling His mission. Peter then adds this fascinating phrase to the end of the passage: "Things which angels desire to look into." Angels serve God, but are not recipients of His salvation.

Why didn't He "call ten thousand angels" to save Him? He had to "finish the work," and glorify His Father in the saving of the lost.

Notice the words of Jesus as He was betrayed into the hands of sinners: "Or do you think that I cannot now pray to My Father, and He will provide Me with more than twelve legions of angels? How then could the Scriptures be fulfilled, that it must happen thus?" (Matthew 26:53–54).

Jesus did not come in the manger and go to the cross to redeem angels. His mission was to save the lost race of mankind. Angels are His creatures, supporting His mission, but humans are the object of His redeeming love, becoming His "new creations" (2 Corinthians 5:17). Only humans can be called to receive Him and become His own children (John 1:12).

So everywhere we find angels we find them busy advancing the mission of Jesus, which is exactly why they stood by and watched their Maker and our Savior die. They are not to be worshiped. Angels were made to worship. You'll always know the true angels of God simply by the fact that they solely advance the worship of Jesus. And they'll be worshiping Him forever.

> *At His feet the six-winged seraph;*
> *cherubim, with sleepless eye,*
> *Veil their faces to the presence,*
> *as with ceaseless voice they cry,*
> *Alleluia, alleluia, alleluia, Lord Most High!*[4]

Psalm 91:11 also tells us that angels protect the saints: "For He shall give His angels charge over you, to keep you in all your ways." Some believers even claim this verse as their spiritual 911 call.[5] And guess who throws a party when a sinner repents and follows Jesus? It's the angels that rejoice (Luke 15:10).

One day King Jesus will return with His mighty host of angels (2 Thessalonians 1:7). Until then, their Christmas celebration never ends! How providential that these rich residents of heaven made their first Christmas Day announcement to "certain poor shepherds in fields as they lay." Touched by the angels, they would never be the same!

Missionary Shepherds

And they came with haste and found Mary and Joseph, and the Babe lying in a manger. Now when they had seen Him, they made widely known the saying which was told them concerning this Child. And all those who heard it marveled at those things which were told them by the shepherds. . . . Then the shepherds returned, glorifying and praising God for all the things that they had heard and seen, as it was told them.

Luke 2:16–18, 20

I once asked my tenth-grade Sunday school class this question: "Can anyone give a good reason why we don't celebrate Christmas every day?" These bright, young rising stars could only come up with such ideas as tradition, wearing out a good thing, running out of food and money for parties, etc. Translation: "Mr. Stu, that's just way too much excitement for every day of the year!"

While Christmas is widely regarded as a season, its biblical practice was anything but seasonal. The shepherds "made haste" to go see Jesus on Christmas Day. They were in a hurry. Most of us get in a big hurry at Christmas, but rarely does our "holiday rush" have to do with seeing and experiencing Jesus.

Suddenly, everything in their lives orbited around the One who holds all things in orbit (Colossians 1:17). We arrange entire rooms around a tree. They arranged their focus on a small feeding trough whose occupant would one day die on a tree.

Christ became the center of their lives immediately—at His birth and after His birth. Christmas for them had only begun. In the most remarkable turn of events, they suddenly became "missionary shepherds" heralding abroad the arrival of the Good Shepherd. Literally everywhere they went they spread the good news. You see, they never got the memo to calm down after Christmas. Come on, boys—"Take down the lights"; "Drag the tree to the curb"; "Box up all the decorations." No, they kept on giving the most valuable gift away—the message of "a Savior, which is Christ the Lord."

How often do we throw around the phrase, "It's the gift that keeps on giving" and "He's the reason for the season all year round"? Try greeting someone with a hearty "Merry Christmas" in January and you may receive a blank, confused reaction. This is exactly why Luke 2:18 says, "And all those who heard it marveled." The people were in awe of what they heard. Certainly they were awestruck by the unlikely source of the news!

How could a message of such eternal import come from such unimportant peasants? These cast-offs of society amazingly became vibrant vessels of life and salvation. They were the first to "go tell it on the mountain." So often at Christmas we sing this famous African American spiritual, created by unknown slaves. Under the oppression of slavery, these godly saints well identified with the humble shepherds. In spite of their bitter state in life, they didn't hoard the message of God's grace, but sang aloud for all to hear. The great comfort and solace they experienced in the good news of the Savior was worth shouting from the mountaintops. John Wesley Work Jr. and his sons refined this legendary song and blessed us all with the version we have today. How wondrous, that truth of "Go Tell It on the Mountain" which began with nameless shepherds and was later faithfully proclaimed to us by nameless slaves. Their song is sung around the world to this day—a universal anthem of the good news found in Jesus Christ!

Down in a lowly manger the humble Christ was born,
and God sent us salvation that blessed Christmas morn.

Later in Jesus's ministry, look who else would be the least qualified, but the most effective evangelists:

- The healed leper published abroad his cleansing (Mark 1:45).
- The adulterous Samaritan woman left her water pot and brought her entire village to Jesus (John 4:1–23).
- The man of Gadarenes went from being an insane, demon-possessed lunatic to the first evangelist in his village (Mark 5:1–20).

- The blind man healed by Jesus preached to the religious leaders, saying, "I was blind, now I see" (John 9:25).
- Zaccheus, the despised tax collector, reached his entire household (Luke 19:9).

Unwrapping the Gift

Jesus is referred to throughout the New Testament as God's gift:

- "For God so loved the world that He gave His only begotten Son" (John 3:16).
- "For the wages of sin is death, but the gift of God is eternal life in Christ Jesus our Lord" (Romans 6:23).
- "But God demonstrates His own love toward us, in that while we were still sinners, Christ died for us" (Romans 5:8).
- "By this we know love, because He laid down His life for us. And we also ought to lay down our lives for the brethren" (1 John 3:16).

How does one open such a gift? Some may argue that Jesus is the ultimate gift as a baby. Or even as a toddler. Others clamored to Him as the Galilean Teacher/Healer/ Crowd Feeder. The cross is by far the greatest expression of His becoming our ultimate gift. What about the resurrected or ascended Christ? Yes, He is all of the above! Paul said it beautifully in Colossians 1:13–18:

He has delivered us from the power of darkness and conveyed us into the kingdom of the Son of His love, in whom we have redemption through His blood, the forgiveness of sins.

He is the image of the invisible God, the firstborn over all creation. For by Him all things were created that are in heaven and that are on earth, visible and invisible, whether thrones or dominions or principalities or powers. All things were created through Him and for Him. And He is before all things, and in Him all things consist. And He is the head of the body, the church, who is the beginning, the firstborn from the dead, that in all things He may have the preeminence.

From beginning to end, Jesus Christ is the total package! He comes to us as a babe at Christmas. He comes to us as a young man consumed with His heavenly Father's purpose. He comes to us as Redeemer, dying in our place. And He comes resurrected in victory and glory, crowned King of heaven and earth. "And He shall reign forever and ever . . . King of kings and Lord of lords." His same glory that attracted wise men and transformed shepherds will light up heaven for all eternity: "The city had no need of the sun or of the moon to shine in it, for the glory of God illuminated it. The Lamb is its light" (Revelation 21:23).

Do you know Him? Not just know *about* Him? The shepherds went to Him and were forever changed. The wise men sought Him and found ultimate joy. Will you call out to Jesus today? Will you believe the good news of what He's done for you and receive His perfect gift of life?

Know Him, Make Him Known

Did you know that at the heart of evangelism is the word "angel"? *Angel* literally means "messenger." *Evangel* means "good news." Evangelism is simply proclaiming the good news. The angels brought the good news to the shepherds; the shepherds took the Gospel, or the good news, to others as the first evangelists. Literally, evangelism is to be a good angel—or messenger—of the good news of the Savior. Have you personally experienced the life-changing power of the good news of the Gospel? Have you shared this good news with others?

My favorite Christmas Day devotional is from Oswald Chambers' *My Utmost for His Highest*. Our family reads this every December 25th. First, Chambers richly highlights His birth in history: "Jesus is not man becoming God, but God Incarnate, God coming into human flesh, coming into it from the outside. His life is the Highest and the Holiest entering in at the Lowliest door. Our Lord's birth was an advent."[6]

He then describes the supernatural nature of "His birth in me": "Just as Our Lord came into human history from outside, so He must come into me from outside. Have I allowed my personal human life to become a 'Bethlehem' for the Son

163

of God? I cannot enter into the realm of the Kingdom of God unless I am born from above by a birth totally unlike natural birth."[7]

When Jesus Christ enters the Bethlehem of your life, everything changes. The eternal destiny of the world was all bound up in that bundle of joy gently clutched by a teenage girl. So your destiny depends on what you do with Jesus. Once you know Him, you'll know His peace. Your passion will be to make Him known, until His glorious return. The angel told His disciples only seconds after Jesus ascended into heaven, "This same Jesus, who was taken up from you into heaven, will so come in like manner as you saw Him go into heaven" (Acts 1:11).

> *Who is He that from the grave*
> *Comes to heal and help and save?*
> *Who is He that from His throne*
> *Rules through all the world alone?*
> *'Tis the Lord! O wondrous story!*
> *'Tis the Lord! The King of glory!*
> *At His feet we humbly fall,*
> *Crown Him! Crown Him, Lord of all!*[8]

As the shepherds spread the good news indiscriminately to everyone, so we must take this message to a lost world—as "far as the curse is found." Our world, desperate for hope and peace and healing, needs the Christ of Christmas, the

One who came to the cradle to go to the cross to ultimately wear the crown. Jesus came into this messed-up world and spoke His powerful first words. He's inviting you to know Him personally through His perfect life, death, and resurrection. Once you know Him, His mission will be your greatest joy.

Let us "go out with joy" and spread the greatest story ever told! While there's still time, like the shepherds, we must

> *Go tell it on the mountain,*
> *over the hills and everywhere,*
> *go tell it on the mountain;*
> *that Jesus Christ is born.*[9]

We are called to spread the good news, and we never know how we will be led to do so. In the mid-1800s, the daunting words of Luke 2:7, "no room in the inn," inspired Emily Elliot to pen the now-famous carol "Thou Didst Leave Thy Throne."

Emily passionately served the rescue missions and homeless community in the slums of England. Her heart for the poor and love for the rich gospel message led her to write this hymn for her Sunday school children in order to communicate the story of advent and ultimate redemption. Her story—and ours—demonstrates how lives are changed when Jesus becomes *the* central part of living.

While there was "no room in the inn" that first Christmas

night, the lives of the Christmas characters were miraculously changed forever when "every heart prepared Him room." Joseph died a faithful stepfather. Mary followed her son and Savior to the very end. The shepherds lit the first fuse of good news that ignited the world. The wise men returned home with a treasure greater than any noble caravan could bear.

"Heaven and nature" still sing as the angels continue their Christ-exalting work every day. The Spirit of the Lord moves across the world through His faithful followers, and He "calls one and calls all, to gain His everlasting hall: because, Christ was born to save! Christ was born to save!"

The King will someday return, not in a cradle, not on a cross, but with a crown. When He does, we'll hear again from the angels and every knee will bow. "Behold, He is coming with clouds, and every eye will see Him, even they who pierced Him" (Revelation 1:7).

Those who know Him will rejoice at His glorious return!

When the heavens shall ring and the angels sing
At thy coming to victory,
Let thy voice call me home
Saying, "Yet there is room,
There is room at My side for thee."
My heart shall rejoice, Lord Jesus,
When thou comest and callest for me.[10]

SCRIPTURE REFLECTIONS
ON THE FIRST WORDS OF JESUS

So he answered, "Do not fear, for those who are with us are more than those who are with them." And Elisha prayed, and said, "LORD, I pray, open his eyes that he may see." Then the LORD opened the eyes of the young man, and he saw. And behold, the mountain was full of horses and chariots of fire all around Elisha.

2 Kings 6:16–17

The angel of the LORD encamps all around those who fear Him, and delivers them.

Psalm 34:7

For He shall give His angels charge over you,
To keep you in all your ways.

Psalm 91:11

Seek the LORD while He may be found,
Call upon Him while He is near.
Let the wicked forsake his way,
And the unrighteous man his thoughts;
Let him return to the LORD,
And He will have mercy on him;
And to our God,

For He will abundantly pardon.
"For My thoughts are not your thoughts,
Nor are your ways My ways," says the LORD.
"For as the heavens are higher than the earth,
So are My ways higher than your ways,
And My thoughts than your thoughts."

Isaiah 55:7–9

"Go therefore and make disciples of all the nations, baptizing them in the name of the Father and of the Son and of the Holy Spirit, teaching them to observe all things that I have commanded you; and lo, I am with you always, even to the end of the age." Amen.

Matthew 28:19–20

Then He said to them, "Thus it is written, and thus it was necessary for the Christ to suffer and to rise from the dead the third day, and that repentance and remission of sins should be preached in His name to all nations, beginning at Jerusalem. And you are witnesses of these things. Behold, I send the Promise of My Father upon you; but tarry in the city of Jerusalem until you are endued with power from on high."

Luke 24:46–49

"But you shall receive power when the Holy Spirit has come upon you; and you shall be witnesses to Me in Jerusalem, and in all Judea and Samaria, and to the end of the earth."

Now when He had spoken these things, while they watched, He was taken up, and a cloud received Him out of their sight. And while they looked steadfastly toward heaven as He went up, behold, two men stood by them in white apparel, who also said, "Men of Galilee, why do you stand gazing up into heaven? This same Jesus, who was taken up from you into heaven, will so come in like manner as you saw Him go into heaven."

Acts 1:8–11

If you confess with your mouth the Lord Jesus and believe in your heart that God has raised Him from the dead, you will be saved. For with the heart one believes unto righteousness, and with the mouth confession is made unto salvation.

Romans 10:9–10

How then shall they call on Him in whom they have not believed? And how shall they believe in Him of whom they have not heard? And how shall they hear without a preacher? And how shall they preach unless they are sent? As it is written:
"How beautiful are the feet of those who preach
the gospel of peace,
Who bring glad tidings of good things!"

Romans 10:14–15

GROUP DISCUSSION QUESTIONS

1. How active are angels in the Bible and in redemptive history?

2. Why are the angels such an important part of the Christmas story?

3. Why were the angels silent at the cross?

4. What about the shepherds' lives changed after their encounter with Jesus?

5. Is Christmas the "end/culmination" or just the "beginning"?

6. Why were the shepherds in such a hurry?

7. What happens in my life when my heart becomes a Bethlehem?

ACKNOWLEDGMENTS

Not sure if I should "acknowledge" or "apologize" to so many friends for enduring my Christmas rants and messages. You see,

I've been on a steady 3 year diet of Christmas music, books and sermons. And . . . I'm still enjoying it.

First, a big Merry thank you to Julie, Hope (& Harrison), Gracie, Joy and Faith. We brought Hope (our firstborn) home from the hospital on Christmas Eve 1994, after the doctors had given her only a slim chance of survival. And what Hope she has given so many in her witness for Christ.

My deepest appreciation goes out to Julie, my bride of over 24 years. You're by far the more gifted writer. You've been a rock in our family in the heat of some difficult trials.

This book almost didn't happen, but God worked it out—largely through your remarkable courage.

To my family, friends, and 10th grade Watson-Payne Sunday school class, thank you for putting up with my Christmas spirit all year round-and all those who aided in the great hymnal heist-Jacob, David, Patterson, and Jeff.

Johnny "Christmas" Angell, you were exactly that! Also grateful for all the support of our Truth Network team along the way-Mike, Betsy, Robby, Dennis and Carol.

Anita "Boss lady" Dean-Arnette, chapter 3 is dedicated to you and the awesome 'Moms of The Light'!

Thank you John Cox for coaching me through my writer's block during a most difficult time in your own life. David Johnson, your insights were huge! Uncle Ray St. John, Ralf Walters, Tom Muse,Sam Horn, and the legendary Coach Mel Hankinson you have been True friends 'down the stretch'.

Christmas WILL come early for all of you.

A special word of gratitude goes out to the men who first heard this material in the context of real life and discipleship; the men of "Wednesdays in the Word": Jeff, Speaks, Randy, Kerry, Hank, Rusty, Barrett, Mark, Ruben, Grey, Wes, Hartley, Zack, Justin, Sam, Barrett, Bondy, Mike, Jeremiah, Graham, Kerry, Doug, Scott, David, Jim, Chetwood, Jumper, Carl, Wasielewski, Tim, Brian, Nash, Wes, C.O., Joe, James, Zack, Bowersox, Calhoun, Denny, George, Uncle Ron, Arnold, Daniel, John, Carl, Val, Brian, Sam, Josh, Ralf, Curtis, Grey, Gavin, Chris and the amazing team at Dairio.

Thanks for the strength and support of my new Canaan "iron buddies": Jay, Khalim, Chris, Todd, Frank, John-Mark, Ralf, Eddie, Lou and the whole gang!

Ted Squires you have been a rock!

Team Worthy Inspired—you have been amazing throughout the whole process. Big thanks to Byron Williamson for believing in me from day one. Pamela Clements—you're guidance and wisdom made this book possible. Ramona Richards, thank you for your remarkable editing and direction, and Wayne Hastings, Cat Hoort, Bart and the rest of the team, I'm so grateful for your fresh ideas and support.

Thank you to Carly, Beth, Tabor, Scott, Andy, Troy, Ruben, Rashawn, Jesse, Asa, Mark, Wes, Sanger, Alex, Sam, Roy and Graham for helping with the launch. And I'm very thankful to the many who bought multiple copies to share with others and "go tell it in the mountain!"

First Words of Jesus music will bless many thanks to the brilliant work Richie and Gina Kingsmore and their wonderful cast of vocalists and musicians.

Eternal thanks to Dad and Mom (Stu Sr. and Nancy) for dragging me to every possible Christmas production ever invented. And yes, it stuck! Much of what you've read here first entered my mind at a young age. How remarkable that the things you once dreaded in youth, are the things you look forward most to as a grown-up.

Hang in there dads and moms. Keep sowing seeds of the Gospel into your children—at Christmas and all the year round.

May we all savor the words of Charles Dickens who said, "for it is good to be children sometimes, and never better than at Christmas, when its mighty Founder was a child Himself."

Merry Christmas!

NOTES

Introduction

1. J. I. Packer, *Knowing God* (Downers Grove, IL: Intervarsity Press, 1973), 51.
2. Though the facts are not conclusive, many scholars believe the manger may have been made of stone, possibly carved into the wall of the building.
3. Johann von Rist, "Break Forth, O Beauteous Heavenly Light," 1641.

Chapter 1: The Power of the First Words

1. E.S. Elliot, "Thou Didst Leave Thy Throne," 1864.
2. Dr. Ralph Washington Sockman, quoted in David Jeremiah, *Why the Nativity?* (Carol Stream, IL: Tyndale House, 2006), 43.
3. Edith M. G. Reed, "Infant holy, infant lowly," 1921.
4. Stu Epperson Jr., *Last Words of Jesus* (Franklin, TN: Worthy Publishing, 2015), 131.
5. Charles Wesley, "Hark! The Herald Angels Sing!," 1734.
6. Isaac Watts "Joy to the World," 1719.
7. Author Unknown, "God Rest Ye Merry Gentlemen."
8. Wesley, "Hark! The Herald Angels Sing!"
9. Ace Collins, *Stories behind the Best-Loved Songs of Christmas* (Grand Rapids, MI: Zondervan, 2001), 132--35.

Chapter 2: The Greatest Message to the Lowliest of Messengers

1. Author Unknown, "Go, Tell It on the Mountain."
2. Author Unknown, "The First Noel."
3. Joni Eareckson Tada, et al., *O Come, All Ye Faithful* (Wheaton, IL: Crossway Books, 2001), 67.
4. While Shepherds Watched Their Flocks" by Nahum Tate
5. Joseph Mohr, "Silent Night! Holy Night!."
6. http://www.desiringgod.org/interviews/what-is-god-s-glory. Accessed June 12, 2016.
7. http://www.the-highway.com/plan_Packer.html. Accessed June 12, 2016.
8. John Francis Wade, "O Come, All Ye Faithful," 1751.
9. Reed, "Infant holy, infant lowly."
10. James Montgomery, "Angels from the Realms of Glory," 1816.
11. Benjamin R. Hanby, "Who Is He in Yonder Stall?," 1866.
12. "Heaven Came Down," Words and music by John W. Peterson © 1961
13. Author Unknown, "Angels We Have Heard on High."
14. D. James Kennedy, *The Real Messiah,* (Nashville, TN: Thomas Nelson, 1982), 37.
15. Robert J. Morgan, *Come Let Us Adore Him* (Nashville, TN: Thomas Nelson, 2005), 108.

Chapter 3: Have a Merry, Mary Christmas

1. Collins, *Stories Behind the Best-Loved Songs of Christmas*, 8.
2. https://www.rca.org/resources/heidelbergcatechism. Accessed June 12, 2016.
3. Packer, *Knowing God*, 46.
4. Cecil Frances Humphreys Alexander, "Once in Royal David's City," 1848.
5. J. D. Greear, *Stop Asking Jesus into Your Heart: How to Know for Sure You Are Saved* (Nashville, TN: B&H Publishing, 2013), 52.

6. John Jacob Niles, "I Wonder as I Wander," 1933.
7. Author Unknown, "O Come, O Come, Emmanuel."
8. Stu Epperson Jr., *Words of Life*, 2015.
9. Matthew Bridges, "Crown Him with Many Crowns," 1851.

Chapter 4: The Dark Side of Christmas
1. Tada, *O Come, All Ye Faithful*, 50.
2. Stu Epperson Jr., "Give Me the Cradle Not the Cross," 2016.
3. Charles Wesley, "Come, Thou Long-Expected Jesus," 1745.
4. Placide Cappeau, "O Holy Night," 1847.

Chapter 5: The Wisest Christmas Shoppers
1. James Montgomery, "Angels from the Realms of Glory," 1816.
2. http://www.desiringgod.org/messages/we-have-come-to-worship-him. Accessed June 12, 2016.
3. https://en.wikipedia.org/wiki/Bowing. Accessed June 12, 2016.
4. William C. Dix, "As with Gladness, Men of Old," 1860.
5. Cappeau, "O Holy Night."
6. John H. Hopkins, Jr., "We Three Kings," 1857.
7. Ibid.
8. Ibid.
9. Collins, *Stories behind the Best-Loved Songs of Christmas*, 178.
10. Stu Epperson Jr., 2016.
11. Christina Rosetti, "In the Bleak Midwinter," 1904.
12. William C. Dix "What Child Is This?."

Chapter 6: Purpose-Driven Jesus
1. Elliot, "Thou Didst Leave Thy Throne."
2. Jerry Bridges, *Transforming Grace,* NavPress (1991), p. 10.
3. http://www.ligonier.org/blog/jesus-and-his-active-obedience/. Accessed June 12, 2016.
4. C. S. Lewis, *The Problem of Pain* (San Francisco: HarperSanFrancisco, 1940, repr., 2001), 91.
5. Heinrich Suso, "Good Christian Men, Rejoice."

Chapter 7: 'Twas the Day After Christmas
1. Stu Epperson Jr., 2016.
2. Johnann Scheffler, "Morning Star, O Cheering Sight," 1657.
3. Robert Morgan, *The Angel Answer Book* (Nashville: Thomas Nelson, 2015), 68.
4. Liturgy of St. James, 5th century.
5. Morgan, *The Angel Answer Book,* 97.
6. Oswald Chambers, *My Utmost for His Highest* (Grand Rapids, MI: Discovery House Publishers, 2010), December 25.
7. Ibid.
8. Benjamin Russell Hanby, "Who Is He in Yonder Stall?," 1866.
9. Author Unknown, "Go, Tell It on the Mountain."
10. Elliot, "Thou Didst Leave Thy Throne."

FOR FURTHER STUDY ON
CHRIST'S FIRST WORDS

A vast amount of material exists on the *First Words of Jesus*. Following is a list of many—but certainly not all—works specifically dedicated to this subject. Additional resources can be found online at FirstWordsofJesus.com.

Bisagno, John. *The Word Made Flesh*. Waco, Texas: Word Books, Copyright 1975 by Word Incorporated.

Boice, James Montgomery. *The Christ of Christmas*. Phillipsburg, New Jersey: Copyright 2009 by Linda M. Boice (previously issued 1983 Moody Press) Reissued 2009 by P & R Publishing.

Boice, James Montgomery. *The King Has Come*. Scotland, Great Britain: Christian Focus Publications Ltd, Copyright 1992 James Montgomery Boice.

Bridges, Jerry. *Transforming Grace: living confidently in God's unfailing love*. Colorado Springs, Colorado: NavPress, Copyright 1991 by Jerry Bridges.

Chappell, Paul. *Christmas Is A Gift*. Lancaster, CA: Striving Together Publications, Copyright 2011 by Striving Together Publications.

Collins, Ace. *Stories Behind the Best-Loved Songs of Christmas*. Grand Rapids, Michigan: Zondervan, Copyright 2001 by Andrew Collins.

Emurian, Ernest K. *Stories of Christmas Carols*. Grand Rapids, Michigan: Baker Books, Copyright1958,1967 by Baker Book House Company, Cloth edition published 1996.

Greear, J. D. *Stop Asking Jesus Into Your Heart how to know for sure you are saved*. Nashville, Tennessee: B & H Publishing Group, Copyright 2013 by J. D. Greear.

Gromacki, Robert Glenn. *The Virgin Birth*. Nashville, Tennessee: Thomas Nelson, Inc, Copyright 1974 by Robert Glenn Gromacki.

Hanegraaff, Hank. *The Heart of Christmas A Devotional for the Season*. Nashville, Tennessee: Thomas Nelson, Copyright 2009 by Hank Hanegraaff.

Jeremiah, David. *Why the Nativity?* Carol Stream, Illinois: Tyndale House Publishers, Inc., Copyright 2006 by David P. Jeremiah.

Kennedy, Ph.D., D. James and Jerry Newcombe, D. Min. *The Real Messiah: Prophecies Fulfilled*. Boca Raton, FL: D. James Kennedy Foundation, Copyright The D. James Kennedy Foundation and Dr. Jerry Newcombe (no specific date listed).

MacArthur, John. *God in the Manger The Miraculous Birth of Christ*. Nashville, Tennessee: W Publishing Group, Copyright 2001 W Publishing Group.

MacArthur, John, Joni Eareckson Tada, Robert & Bobbie Wolgemuth. *O Come, All Ye Faithful.* Wheaton, Illinois: Crossway Books, Copyright 2001.

MacArthur, John F., Jr. *The Miracle of Christmas* previously published as *God With Us.* Grand Rapids, Michigan: Zondervan Publishing House, Copyright 1995 by John F. MacArthur, Jr. Previously published as God With Us: The Miracle of Christmas This new edition published in 1993.

Machen, J. Gresham. *The Virgin Birth Of Christ.* Grand Rapids, Michigan: Baker Book House, Copyright 1930 by Harper & Row, Publishers, Incorporated Reprinted by Baker Book House Company with special permission Fourth printing, April 1974.

(many various authors). *The Incarnation An Anthology.* Nashville, Tennessee: Thomas Nelson, Inc., Copyright 2002 by Thomas Nelson, Inc.

McLaughlin, David. *Silent Night: the stories behind 40 beloved Christmas carols.* Uhrichsville, Ohio: Barbour Publishing, Inc, Copyright 2013 by Barbour Publishing, Inc.

Morgan, Robert J. *The Angel Answer Book.* Nashville, Tennessee: Thomas Nelson, Copyright 2015 by Robert J. Morgan.

Morgan, Robert J. *Come Let Us Adore Him Stories Behind the Most Cherished Christmas Hymns.* Nashville, Tennessee: Thomas Nelson, Copyright 2005 by Robert J. Morgan.

Osbeck, Kenneth W. *101 Hymn Stories.* Grand Rapids, Michigan: Kregel Publications, Copyright 1982 by Kregel Publications.

Packer, J. I. *Knowing God.* Downers Grove, Illinois: InterVarsity Press, Copyright 1973 by J. I. Packer, Ninth American printing, June 1976.

Pearce, J. Winston. *Seven First Words Of Jesus.* Nashville, Tennessee: Broadman Press, 1966.

Peterson, Schuyler. *Five First Words Of Jesus.* Publisher unknown, requests for more information should be addressed to: Southside Baptist Church, c/o Dr. Schuyler Peterson, 316 South Church Street, Spartanburg, SC 29306, Copyright 2015 by Schuyler Peterson.

Rogers, Adrian. *A Family Christmas Treasury.* Wheaton, Illinois: Crossway Books, Copyright 1997 by Adrian Rogers.

Inspirational Writings from Swindoll, Charles, Max Lucado, Charles Colson. *The Glory of Christmas.* Dallas, Texas: Word Publishing, Copyright 1996 by Word Publishing, Inc.

Verbrugge, Verlyn D. *A Not-So-Silent Night: the unheard story of Christmas and why it matters.* Grand Rapids, MI: Kregel Publications, Copyright 2009 by Verlyn D. Verbrugge.

ABOUT THE AUTHOR

Stu Epperson Jr., BA, MS, is the author of *Last Words of Jesus: First Steps to a Richer Life*, and founder and president of the Truth Network with radio stations across North Carolina, central Iowa, and Salt Lake City. Truth Network also develops and syndicates programs on over three hundred affiliates nationwide. In his spare time Stu hosts *Truth Talk Live*, his own nationally syndicated show, and he coaches and mentors through the game of basketball. His passion is that all people everywhere will experience truth. Stu lives in North Carolina, with his family.

Visit and follow Stu Epperson Jr. at

FirstWordsofJesus.com

 facebook.com/stu.epperson

 twitter.com/@stuepperson
#FirstWordsofJesus

 instagram.com/ @stuepperson

STEPS TO PEACE WITH GOD

1. GOD'S PURPOSE: PEACE AND LIFE

God loves you and wants you to experience peace and life—abundant and eternal.

THE BIBLE SAYS ...

"We have peace with God through our Lord Jesus Christ." *Romans 5:1, NKJV*

"For God so loved the world that He gave His only begotten Son, that whoever believes in Him should not perish but have everlasting life." *John 3:16, NKJV*

"I have come that they may have life, and that they may have it more abundantly." *John 10:10, NKJV*

Since God planned for us to have peace and the abundant life right now, why are most people not having this experience?

2. OUR PROBLEM: SEPARATION FROM GOD

God created us in His own image to have an abundant life. He did not make us as robots to automatically love and obey Him, but gave us a will and a freedom of choice.

We chose to disobey God and go our own willful way. We still make this choice today. This results in separation from God.

THE BIBLE SAYS ...

"For all have sinned and fall short of the glory of God." *Romans 3:23, NKJV*

"For the wages of sin is death, but the gift of God is eternal life in Christ Jesus our Lord." *Romans 6:23, NKJV*

Our choice results in separation from God.

People (Sinful) God (Holy)

OUR ATTEMPTS

Through the ages, individuals have tried in many ways to bridge this gap ... without success ...

THE BIBLE SAYS ...

"There is a way that seems right to a man, but its end is the way of death."
Proverbs 14:12, NKJV

"But your iniquities have separated you from your God; and your sins have hidden His face from you, so that He will not hear."
Isaiah 59:2, NKJV

There is only one remedy for this problem of separation.

3. GOD'S REMEDY: THE CROSS

Jesus Christ is the only answer to this problem. He died on the cross and rose from the grave, paying the penalty for our sin and bridging the gap between God and people.

THE BIBLE SAYS ...

"For there is one God and one Mediator between God and men, the Man Christ Jesus."
1 Timothy 2:5, NKJV

"For Christ also suffered once for sins, the just for the unjust, that He might bring us to God."
1 Peter 3:18, NKJV

"But God shows his love for us in that while we were still sinners, Christ died for us." *Romans 5:8, ESV*

God has provided the only way ... we must make the choice ...

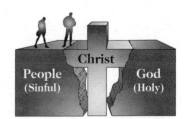

4. OUR RESPONSE: RECEIVE CHRIST

We must trust Jesus Christ and receive Him by personal invitation.

THE BIBLE SAYS ...

"Behold, I stand at the door and knock. If anyone hears My voice and opens the door, I will come in to him and dine with him, and he with Me." *Revelation 3:20, NKJV*

"But to all who did receive him, who believed in his name, he gave the right to become children of God." *John 1:12, ESV*

"If you confess with your mouth that Jesus is Lord and believe in your heart that God raised him from the dead, you will be saved." *Romans 10:9, ESV*

Are you here ... or here?

Is there any good reason why you cannot receive Jesus Christ right now?

HOW TO RECEIVE CHRIST:

1. Admit your need (say, "I am a sinner").
2. Be willing to turn from your sins (repent) and ask for God's forgiveness.
3. Believe that Jesus Christ died for you on the cross and rose from the grave.
4. Through prayer, invite Jesus Christ to come in and control your life through the Holy Spirit (receive Jesus as Lord and Savior).

WHAT TO PRAY:

Dear God,

    I know that I am a sinner. I want to turn from my sins, and I ask for Your forgiveness. I believe that Jesus Christ is Your Son. I believe He died for my sins and that You raised Him to life. I want Him to come into my heart and to take control of my life. I want to trust Jesus as my Savior and follow Him as my Lord from this day forward.

In Jesus' Name, amen.

_____   _____

Date   Signature

GOD'S ASSURANCE: HIS WORD

IF YOU PRAYED THIS PRAYER,

THE BIBLE SAYS ...

"For 'everyone who calls on the name of the Lord will be saved.'"
Romans 10:13, ESV

Did you sincerely ask Jesus Christ to come into your life? Where is He right now? What has He given you?

"For by grace you have been saved through faith. And this is not your own doing; it is the gift of God, not a result of works, so that no one may boast." *Ephesians 2:8–9, ESV*

THE BIBLE SAYS ...

"He who has the Son has life; he who does not have the Son of God does not have life. These things I have written to you who believe in the name of the Son of God, that you may know that you have eternal life, and that you may continue to believe in the name of the Son of God."
1 John 5:12–13, NKJV

Receiving Christ, we are born into God's family through the supernatural work of the Holy Spirit, who indwells every believer. This is called regeneration or the "new birth."

This is just the beginning of a wonderful new life in Christ. To deepen this relationship you should:

1. Read your Bible every day to know Christ better.
2. Talk to God in prayer every day.
3. Tell others about Christ.
4. Worship, fellowship, and serve with other Christians in a church where Christ is preached.
5. As Christ's representative in a needy world, demonstrate your new life by your love and concern for others.

God bless you as you do.

Franklin Graham

If you want further help in the decision you have made, write to:
Billy Graham Evangelistic Association
1 Billy Graham Parkway, Charlotte, NC 28201-0001

1-877-2GRAHAM (1-877-247-2426)
BillyGraham.org/commitment